# BEYOND HELLO

## Rekindling the Human Spirit

## One Conversation at a Time

### By Kristi Blakeway

Beyond Hello: Rekindling the Human Spirit One Conversation at a Time

As You Wish Publishing, LLC
Kyra@asyouwishpublishing.com 602-592-1141
www.asyouwishpublishing.com

ISBN-13: 978-1-951131-91-3
ISBN-10: 1-951131-91-6
Library of Congress Control Number: 2019914051

Edited by Todd Schaefer

Printed in the United States of America.

Nothing in this book or any affiliations with this book is a substitute for medical or psychological help. If you are needing help please seek it. Each paperback book sold buys a meal for someone in need.

*To Cindy*

*Thank you for teaching me to believe in miracles.*

*It's an honor to be your friend.*

*Kristi*

# Table of Contents

# Foreword By Selina Robinson

Just like Kristi, my life changed because I chose to engage with strangers. Instead of directly engaging as she did, I chose a different path. I chose to speak at a Coquitlam council meeting in support of a temporary homeless shelter that would be in a church around the corner from my suburban house, a half a block from where Kristi was a school counselor. I never anticipated how that one action, to speak up on behalf of those in our community that had been marginalized, ignored, disenfranchised and forgotten, would eventually lead to a seat on Coquitlam City Council (2008), then to a seat as a member of the BC Legislative Assembly (2013) and in 2017, to become BC's Minister of Housing—responsible for addressing a significant housing crisis in the province as well as a homelessness crisis that had been growing for well over a decade.

These stories that you are about to read serve to remind us all that everybody that we see covered in newspapers, sleeping bags, blankets and tarps—whether they are in our parks, ravines, doorways or city streets—is more than a body. Kristi's commitment to listening to people as they share their stories about who they are, where they come from and who they want to be touches upon the humanity of those who have been forgotten.

Kristi reminds us that these people are mothers and fathers; sisters and brothers; grandparents, children, friends and neighbors. She reminds us not to judge and to be accepting when we meet someone who is different. She reminds us that we can each make a difference in the lives of others.

As you read these stories about people who never asked to be broken, homeless, drug addicted, mentally ill, or forgotten; remember their humanity, remember to be kind and remember their hope; their hope for redemption, forgiveness and new possibilities.


Selina Robinson

BC Minister of Housing

.

# Introduction

I grew up talking to strangers. As a child, I thought this was typical. I had no idea that most parents warned their children never to do such a thing. Perhaps my interest in meeting new people came from my confident single mother who served as a teacher by day and the owner of a catering company by night, or perhaps it came from my warm-hearted grandparents who believed every stranger was a friend they had yet to meet. Maybe my willingness to connect came from my need for approval filling the void of my absent father.

Regardless, some of my most memorable moments come from talking to strangers. At age nine, following the advice of my mother, I jumped from our car on a dark, rainy night to cross a busy intersection to help an elderly man pick up a parcel. The next two minutes felt like an eternity as I desperately waited for the light to change while the intoxicated man staggered and swung at me with his bottle wrapped in a sopping wet, paper bag. At thirteen, I accepted an invitation to sit with a boy with Autism and have lunch in the high school cafeteria while my friends stared with wonder. That moment was the beginning of the most joyous friendship I have ever known. At fourteen, I approached a girl from California, standing alone on the first day of school and asked if she would like to be friends. Years later, she was the maid-of-honor at my wedding. At fifteen, my outgoing and exuberant personality mixed with some teenage bravado gave me the confidence to approach a stranger and suggest he ask my mom out on a date. They were married within months, and for the last thirty years, he has been my step-dad.

So, perhaps it comes as no surprise that in November of 2009, as I was reading the local newspaper, an idea hit me that included the simple act of talking to strangers. As a teacher, I was hoping to find ways for my students to give back to the community. That particular year, I had a group of exceptional leadership students who had an incredible sense of compassion and social justice. It was a challenge to keep them fulfilled as they had so much enthusiasm and willingness to give. Our goal was to make a positive difference in the school and the community. We decided we wanted to help the homeless.

Vancouver is home to Canada's poorest neighborhood. Within six city blocks, thousands of people live on the streets. This area is known as the Downtown Eastside (DTES). The school I was working for at the time is located 30 minutes outside Vancouver in the suburbs. Homelessness had become a local issue and the first shelter program had just opened, operating out of local churches. We knew it was time to offer our help.

My students and I began volunteering in the local shelter offering dinner service and conversation. We also made plans to take food and clothing to the less fortunate living on the streets of Vancouver. As I read the weekend paper that Sunday morning, I noticed a series entitled *Operation Phoenix* outlining all of the service agencies helping the homeless on Vancouver's streets. As Christmas approached, many organizations were overlapping services and handouts were in abundance. I decided to cancel our day of giving. My students were devastated. I sat with this complexity: If our desire was to help, and the service was already being provided, why were we disappointed? We realized that *we* wanted to experience the joy of giving. This led to a deeper question: *Do the homeless ever have the chance to give to others?*

Rather than handing out food and clothing, we developed *Project HELLO (Helping Everyone Locate Loved Ones)* and we began to make handmade greeting cards so that the homeless had something to give. As a young mom of two toddlers, I had limited spare time and my craft room had become a thing of the past. I had boxes of cardstocks, stamps and decorative paper tucked away in storage. I invited my students to make blank greeting cards so we could talk to strangers.

With guarded optimism, my students and I headed to the streets in 2009, not knowing what to expect. We hoped people would engage in conversation and possibly take our cards to give away, or to reach out to loved ones. We offered to mail cards, free of charge. Magic began to happen, and one by one, people who had not spoken with family for years opened up and shared their stories. The homeless wrote to their children, their parents, their friends and their siblings, and they trusted us with their messages, dreams and fears. One by one, my students began to help people connect. We searched phone directories and the internet to find families. In our first few years, we made hundreds of connections finding families across Canada and the United States.

By 2013, I recognized that some of the personal stories we were hearing were so raw, that our quick five-minute conversations were not enough. I began what I call *Beyond HELLO* and made the personal commitment to take a homeless person to lunch each month to hear their story.

I have spent a decade talking to strangers on the street. There is a certain wisdom that comes from those who have lost it all. Rock bottom is a solid foundation that allows a true opportunity to recognize what matters. While I started out with the intention of giving to others, I have gained more than I could have ever imagined. Connecting with compassion has helped me heal my soul. We are all here to connect. We are not meant to live this life alone.

I encourage everyone to go *Beyond HELLO. Beyond HELLO* means more than talking to the homeless. It means taking time in our fast-paced world to stop and engage in soulful dialogue. It means seeing people for who they are and understanding that each of us has a story worth hearing. *Beyond HELLO* means living with awareness and recognizing that nothing is more important or meaningful than human connection.

I am grateful to the courageous men and women who have trusted me with their stories. I believe I have been given their stories as a gift, and with them, I hold the responsibility to find meaning and share their stories with you. Perhaps as you read their stories, you will think of a neighbor you have yet to meet or the shop owner you smile at on your way to work. Perhaps you will find the courage to reach out and connect with a friend or relative you have lost touch with. Perhaps you will see the world through different eyes and suspend judgment, recognizing that we are all more alike than different. I hope this book will resonate with your life, and that the universe will whisper to you giving you the confidence you need to go *Beyond HELLO*. What started out as a one-day field trip has turned into my life's greatest purpose. Together, let's go *Beyond HELLO* and rekindle the human spirit, one conversation at a time.


With love,

Kristi

# SECTION

## PRECONCEIVED NOTIONS

*"There is no darkness—but ignorance."*
*William Shakespeare*

# Chapter 1
## Shifting Perceptions

*"Change your perception, change your life."* Anonymous

***Milwaukee Fire – Meeting Irvin – November 2009***

I am embarrassed to say I once judged the homeless with my preconceived notions. Like many, I assumed most of the people in homeless shelters had made bad decisions, or let addiction ruin their lives. I assumed most were out of work, or not motivated to find a job. Without giving it much thought, I somehow assumed that homeless people were different than me. When I signed up to help at the shelter with my students, I had a false sense of superiority or a savior complex thinking we would swoop in and help the less fortunate. I had no idea they would help us.

In the fall of 2009, I began working with my high school students in a local homeless shelter, one block from our school. The idea of a shelter was new to our community, and nobody wanted the homeless in their neighborhood, so the city reached a compromise where the shelter location rotated every month. Local churches of various denominations opened their doors between 10 PM and 7 AM and invited the homeless in for a night's rest. Despite Vancouver's unpredictable weather, the community only supported the idea of a neighborhood shelter between the months of October through March. From April through September, those without housing were expected to live on the streets or on the trails.

# CHAPTER 1 | SHIFTING PERCEPTIONS

The shelter program invited school groups or community agencies to sign up for shifts and provide meals and conversation in the evening or first thing in the morning. Together, with my team of tenth-grade leadership students, we decided to volunteer twice a week for the winter months. Our goal as a leadership group was to make a positive difference in the school and the community and this was our way of giving back. Our intention was to serve. My students expected little more than some volunteer experience to list on their resumes or college applications. My mom, Karen, and our school principal, Mary, offered to help prepare the meals, and the students and teachers offered to help serve dinner to the homeless. Little did we know, this simple act would change us all. We set out to give, but we were about to gain more than we could ever imagine.

With hope and optimism, we prepared for our first shift at the shelter. My mom made chicken pot pie and dinner rolls followed by raspberry crumble and ice-cream. We arrived at the church, expecting to find a mock shelter. In my ignorance, I assumed the shelter would have beds. I was startled to learn that the homeless were only given a thin mat to use while sleeping on the hard floor. Shelter occupants were not able to enter the building until 10 PM. Upon arrival, they were given their thin mat, a sleeping bag and a pillow for the floor. They were invited to eat a homemade dinner followed by lights out at 11 PM. At 6 AM, all those using the shelter needed to rise, tidy their space, grab a quick breakfast and bagged lunch and be back out on the streets by 7 AM. There was no shower.

Shocked by the lack of amenities, my students and I timidly prepared dinner, not knowing what to expect of the shelter guests. We didn't know anyone homeless. What would they be like? After delivering plated meals to the tables, my students and I sat down to join in the conversation.

Irvin was the first homeless person we met. Irvin had the stereotypical image of a street person: his clothes were worn and dirty, his hair unruly, and he was unshaven. His hands suggested a life of manual labor and his shoulders hinted that life had not been easy. Irvin's blue eyes sparkled, and he offered kindness and gratitude as we engaged in conversation. His rough exterior disguised his gentle interior. Irvin told us that it was his mom's birthday. I asked him if he had called her, thinking that perhaps he would want to use my cell phone to say hello. Irvin smiled and let me know his mom had long since passed.

"I guess you didn't get to talk to her then," I offered.

"Actually, I talk to her every day," Irvin began. "I've lost two sisters and my mom, but I take time every day to speak to them in heaven."

I found the courage to ask Irvin about his sisters, suspecting that they had passed recently of natural causes. Irvin was in his sixties, so perhaps his sisters were older and had lived a good life.

Irvin paused as he ate his chicken pot pie and put his cutlery aside to share his story—a story I will never forget. Irvin spoke of his childhood in Milwaukee and a horrific night when he was only six years old. Living in poverty, with a single mom and three siblings, he awoke to find their house on fire. Irvin woke one sister who shared a room with him. He then ran across the hall to try and get to the room his other two sisters shared. The fire blocked the entrance, so he ran to wake his mom. He shared his memory of his mom running into the fire, trying to save her daughters. He then recalled the image of his mom emerging from the house covered in burns and overcome with grief as she whispered, "They are gone."

In that moment, Irvin lost a 3-year-old and 8-year-old sister. Fifty years later, this image has not faded. It is forever burned into his brain, overshadowing his life with pain and tragedy. Trying to hold back my tears, I told Irvin he was a hero for saving his mom and one sister. He smiled in appreciation and he glanced at me for a second as if to consider forgiveness, but the guilt quickly returned, and his face told me my words were not enough—the pain was still too raw. He politely excused himself to go for a cigarette and I excused myself to tidy up the kitchen.

As Irvin rose from his chair, the other guests in unison honored him with a friendly saying: "Cowboy up!" In that moment, I realized I knew nothing about homelessness. I had judged Irvin, thinking his life was a result of his actions, yet hearing his story made me realize that Irvin was a grown man, stuck in the trauma of his childhood. Decades later, he had learned life the hard way, sleeping in the woods. To the others on the streets, Irvin was their protector, their friend, and a man of courage and composure. Kind and well respected, Irvin was known for his engineering and mechanical skills. He was their cowboy. It became immediately obvious that Irvin was loved by many but struggled to love himself.

As we finished the dishes, and the homeless guests set up their sleeping quarters, a wave of silence settled over the kitchen. Irvin was not the person we had expected to meet. As I waited for parents to pick up their teens, one boy looked lost in thought. I asked if he was okay. With sincerity, he offered this:

*For the past year, I have been feeling sorry for myself because my parents are getting divorced. Tonight, I met so many people who have lost everything and experienced trauma greater than anything I have ever known. I see now how lucky I am to have two parents who love me who happen to live in two homes.*

It was the first time I noticed the impact our work was having on my students. I realized we were not just helping the homeless—they were helping us.

As I drove home, I cried. I thought of my new home with my loving husband and young sons, age four and age two, curled up in their beds, fast asleep. I thought of all I took for granted, and how fortunate I was to have my family intact, peaceful, and together.

### Trusting School Again – Dinner with Charlie – November 2009

As winter set in, demand for the shelter grew, and my students and I continued to get to know the homeless in our community. In mid-November, I sat down beside Charlie at dinner. There was little doubt Charlie was homeless. He was dirty and unshaven and had a lingering smell of alcohol on his breath. He seemed street smart but unable to conquer his addiction. He was the type most would judge by his appearance. Charlie was curious about my leadership students who were volunteering late at night or early in the morning to help him and others. He was impressed that teenagers would volunteer and expect nothing in return. I then pointed out that the chef in the kitchen was our high school principal. He could not believe it. This was not his view of a high school principal. When he grew up, the principal was the disciplinarian. Charlie believed his principal had lacked compassion and cared more about rules than students themselves.

A minute later, Charlie lowered his voice and whispered to me, "See this?"

At the same time, he made a slight gesture and gently slid his dinner knife forward by an inch along the plastic tabletop. Feeling like I was living a scene from *Prison Break* I whispered back, "Your knife?"

"Yup. Got myself into trouble taking one of these into the principal's office!"

"I imagine that didn't turn out well."

"Not so much."

"I'm assuming you mean when you were a student in high school?"

"No, as a parent. That man touched my boy. My son came home and told me what happened. No one believed me. The cops said I was a simple drunk. But one year later I was watching the news and that same man was arrested for molesting two more boys. I had told them, but they didn't believe me."

I could see that Charlie was reliving pain he could not move past. Again, I recognized that homelessness is about so much more than financial struggles; it is about pain, emotional suffering and disconnection from loved ones. Charlie was stuck—and life had moved on without him.

As Christmas was approaching, I asked Charlie if he would see his family. His eyes lit up as he spoke of his beautiful granddaughter. He spoke of how proud he was to have her in his life. He explained that when he is sober, his daughter lets him walk his granddaughter to her elementary school. Looking at the state of Charlie, I doubted whether he really walked on and off the elementary school grounds each morning, but I was happy that Charlie believed this to be true.

The next morning, I had a meeting to attend so I left home a little later than normal. As I drove along the highway around 8:30 AM, I noticed a man walking with purpose. As I slowed for the red light, I glanced over only to see Charlie on his way to school with his granddaughter. Hand in hand they walked, ready for a new day. This time, Charlie walked towards school with a smile. As I sat at the light, I cried, ashamed of my ignorance. I had judged Charlie and didn't believe he would follow through with his responsibilities as a grandparent. I smiled, finding some comfort that Charlie had learned to trust school again.

*"Love is the absence of judgment." Dalai Lama*

## Chapter 2
## Broken Connections

*"The love of a family is life's greatest blessing."*
*Anonymous*

### Hallway Tears

My first childhood memory is one of my parents arguing in our front hallway. I was four years old, and my parents yelled back and forth, standing roughly five feet from one another. The foyer was lined with floor to ceiling mirrors, so I could see my reflection as I ran back and forth between their legs, not knowing which parent to hang onto as the argument continued. It is my only memory of my parents together, and my only memory where I loved my parents equally. At four years old, I was oblivious to my dad's unfaithfulness, lies and deceit. I was far too young to understand why my mom had found the courage to ask him to leave. All I knew was that the two people who loved me no longer seemed to like each other. It was the beginning of my life with divorced parents.

From that moment forward, my memories of my mom include love, adventure and family. My memories with my dad include cancelled visits, missed phone calls and excuses as to why he couldn't find time for my brother or me. Missed weekend visits became missed months as my dad came in and out of our lives, never making us a priority. Eventually, thirteen years later, after two additional failed marriages, more affairs, job loss and bankruptcy, my dad ruined almost every relationship he had and became homeless.

9

In my late teens, after watching a moving episode of *Oprah*, I found the courage to tell my dad I was no longer willing to be mistreated, or emotionally abused. I would no longer listen to his fake promises or lies about the harm we had caused him. I wouldn't accept that his marriages had ended because he talked about us too much. Enough was enough, so I said goodbye.

To this day, I do not regret the decision to end the relationship with my dad, as saying no to him was my way of saying yes to myself. My younger brother Jeff who has a heart of gold and much more patience than me, continued to try to maintain a relationship with him for years. Once or twice a year, our dad would pop into my brother's life and suggest they meet for a game of golf. (Our dad had mastered the art of breaking into golf courses through holes in the fences to avoid paying.) Each time, Jeff would get his clubs ready only to be disappointed as my dad would not show. This heartbreaking charade continued all through our adult lives until my dad passed away in 2016.

I have come to realize that my dad's absence was a gift in disguise. Our childhood was fantastic, growing up with cousins, aunts, uncles, grandparents and my mom as a huge circle of support. Having one parent who was loving and thoughtful and the other who was absent and neglectful helped me become who I am today. Their polar opposite parenting styles helped me figure out what I loved and what I hated. From my mom, I gained confidence and courage, and from my dad's mistreatment, I gained a sense of empathy and compassion for others as I could relate to their pain. Sometimes, what is missing from your life becomes your greatest asset. My dad failed to show us love or connection, and in turn, those values became increasingly important to me. Despite the joy and pain of my childhood, I am grateful for each experience. It's exactly why I have the courage, compassion and creativity to reach out and help others. It helped me understand everyone has a story worth hearing.

### *Day One of Project HELLO – November 2009*

I'll never forget the day I had the idea for *Project HELLO* (*Helping Everyone Locate Loved Ones*). It was a Sunday morning, and I was reading the morning newspaper. The *Vancouver Province* was running a series on homelessness discussing the merits of the social programs offering assistance. There were hundreds of organizations offering help, and all seemed to focus on food or shelter. It had become almost trendy for church and school groups to run coat drives and take their collections to the cold streets of Vancouver. The homeless, living within six city blocks, were not only suffering from poverty and addiction, but they were also becoming a Christmas novelty. Do-gooders were practically tripping over one another to be able to say they were helping at Christmas. Something felt wrong. I knew I could not take my students. I cancelled our field trip.

I sat with this dilemma for a while. My students would be disappointed they could not help, but the need was being met. So why the disappointment? Like others racing to the streets, we wanted to feel the joy that comes from helping. Our good deeds were as much about us as they were about others. Giving allowed us to experience happiness. I became curious. Do the homeless get to experience this? *Do the homeless ever have the chance to give to others*? My idea was born. We would not give away food and clothing. We would give away the 'power of giving.'

I picked up the phone and called my mom. In an excited tone (the same one I used years earlier to set her up on the blind date where she met my step-dad), I told her I had a new idea!

"Mom, listen to this. I have an idea. Do you know how everyone else gives the homeless food or clothing? What if I use all my scrapbooking supplies and make blank Christmas cards with my students and invite the homeless to give cards away to their friends on the street? We could ask people to write to their families and maybe we could even help someone find family they have lost touch with! What do you think?"

"Honey, it sounds like a nice idea. I'm out for brunch so I have to go. But don't you think the homeless would call their family themselves if they wanted to?"

Awe, Mom. You made my spark a little brighter. I love my mom dearly, but I will always hold onto an ounce of rebelliousness and a strong need for independence. When my mom says think twice, I hear 'Go.'

I loaded up my scrapbooking supplies and called a meeting with my student leaders. It was time to head to the streets and talk to strangers to see what would happen.

### The Heart of the Community – Noelle – November 30, 2009

On November 30th, 2009, we headed to the streets not knowing what to expect. Santa had arrived at local shopping malls, but no one was in the Christmas spirit along Hastings

Street, Canada's most notorious area for homelessness. The weather was cold and damp, and thousands of Vancouver's marginalized citizens lined the sidewalks, as commuters raced by oblivious of their existence.

With trepidation, my students and I began approaching people one by one asking if they would like to send any Christmas cards. For many, it was their first thought of Christmas for this season. When you have lost touch with family and live on the streets, Christmas does not always evoke happy memories. Some politely said no, others seemed slightly annoyed, and some said yes.

The first lady we met was a woman named Noelle. Noelle appeared fragile, standing with a cane for support and wrapped in clothing far too big for her five-foot frame. There was something different about Noelle. While others seemed stressed, Noelle looked at peace. Her smile lit up the neighborhood, and it was immediately obvious she was known and loved by the people on the streets. In the Downtown Eastside (DTES), Canada's poorest neighborhood, she was known as 'Little Mamma,' the heart of the community.

We asked Noelle if she would like to send a Christmas card to any friends or family. She paused at first, not wanting to inconvenience us, and then spoke softly, "I'd like to write a card to my daughter and grandchildren. I haven't heard from them in over ten years."

Noelle sifted through the student-made Christmas cards to find one her grandchildren would like.

She began to write:

*"Dear Natalie and Kids,*

*I love you, I miss you and I hope to see you soon.*

*Hugs and Kisses,*

*Noelle (mom)"*

We promised Noelle we would do what we could to find her daughter, Natalie, knowing only that she had lived in Alberta ten years ago. Noelle knew her daughter had three children back then, but she was not sure if more grandchildren had been born since their last conversation.

Later that afternoon, I returned to my job as a high school counselor. It was a busy afternoon, and the line of students and phone calls left little time for *Project HELLO*. We had five written cards from our first day on the streets and my heart was aching to search for families. Between appointments, I reached into the bag and pulled out Noelle's card. I eagerly searched online phone directories for anyone with a matching surname in Alberta. I began to call wrong numbers. A handful of calls in, a woman answered. I politely asked for Natalie.

"Sorry, Natalie isn't home right now. Can I take a message?"

Stunned, I replied, "You mean this is the right number? Natalie lives with you?"

"Yes, I am her roommate. She will be home soon. Can I help you?"

"Do you happen to know if she has a mom in Vancouver?"

"Yes! She traveled to Vancouver last year to find her mom and couldn't find her. She has been searching for five years now! She assumed her mom had passed away!"

"Please have her call me. Her mom is alive and wants to see her and I have a Christmas card that she has written that I hope to send."

We exchanged details and hung up. I held it together until the phone clicked down. And then, alone in my office, I cried – tears of joy, tears of love, tears of pride for my students and tears for a family whose pain I cannot imagine. I savored the moment knowing we had made a connection. That had been our goal, and if no other connections were made, this would still be a moment I would remember for life.

Hours later, Natalie called, and we had a beautiful conversation. I promised I would head back to the streets to find Noelle to let her know Natalie was doing well. I had no idea how I would find Noelle again, but I knew it was a promise I would keep. I began to realize we had started something more than a one-day school field trip. For the next two weeks, I searched Vancouver's streets whenever I had time hoping to find Noelle. No luck. I had to keep trying.

### *A Card from James – November 30, 2009*

While I knew I had to find Noelle again, I also knew we had other men and women from the streets who had written cards. Switching gears, I focused on a card from James, written to his elderly mother, Margaret.

This time, I had a last name, and I knew that James's mom was located in a small town in Ontario. All I had to do was track down the phone number. I began to call. Five long-distance calls in, I had five wrong numbers. I began to wonder how big the school's long-distance bill would be. I kept calling. On call six, a lady answered and said, *"Yes, this is Margaret."* Feeling like a telemarketer, I introduced myself as a high school teacher and counselor. I explained that my students had been on Hastings Street in Vancouver offering the homeless an opportunity to mail Christmas cards. I let her know that we had met her son, James.

In a soft whisper that bled of love and hurt, she continued, "Yes, James is my son! How is he?"

"He's doing well," I replied. "Many people were not receptive to our program, but your son James was, and he thought of you right away and wanted to send a card."

Margaret went on to explain that James calls about every six months. With Christmas approaching, she had hoped she would hear from him. With shame, Margaret explained to me that she wires him money occasionally. "I know I shouldn't, but he's still my baby." As a mom of a grown man struggling with addiction, she does not know how to help. She told me that no matter how old her son gets, she cannot stop worrying as a mother. I assured her that she is doing the right thing by keeping the lines of communication open. I let her know I would mail the card. We wished each other a Merry Christmas and hung up. Again, I cried. This time I cried for Margaret, I cried as a mother, and I cried at the power of our project.

Before beginning *Project HELLO*, I had never taken the time to think of homeless people's families. What would it be like to lose someone you love to the streets? Despite my struggles with my dad, I had made the conscious decision to end our relationship. What about the sons, daughters, moms and dads who lose a loved one to homelessness and live every day worrying? I was beginning to realize that homelessness was not about a lack of shelter. It was so much more, often symbolic of past trauma and broken connections.

*"Every addiction arises from an unconscious refusal to face and move through your own pain. Every addiction starts with pain and ends with pain. Whatever the substance you are addicted to–alcohol, food, legal or illegal drugs, or a person–you are using something or somebody to cover up your pain."*
*Eckhart Tolle*

# Chapter 3
## Lessons of Hope

*"Only in darkness, can you see the stars."*
*Martin Luther King, Jr.*

### Christmas Miracles – December 2009

By early December of 2009, *Project HELLO* had spun into a Christmas frenzy. My students and I took any chance we could get to return to the Downtown Eastside. We wanted everyone to have the opportunity to give at Christmas. We had 50 families to try and find that first season. December became less about shopping and more about giving, and my students were as invested as I was. Together, we experienced lessons of hope as we helped people write messages of love and then sat for hours in front of computers and phones, trying to create Christmas miracles.

### I Cry for My Son – Winnie – December 18, 2009

One particular evening, my students were having an extraordinary amount of luck phoning and locating families. Family members were excited to hear from loved ones and cards were quickly getting sealed and mailed in time for Christmas. Dini, one of my students, was not having such luck. While it seemed like everyone around her was making connections, she was calling a swarm of wrong numbers. Feeling discouraged, she picked up another card from a man named Wilfred, addressed to a lady named Winnie in Manitoba. After a series of wrong numbers, an elderly lady answered the phone. Dini asked to speak to Winnie. The lady replied, "Sorry dear, I can't hear you…. No, there is no one here named Vern." Winnie hung up. Rather than discounting

CHAPTER 3 | LESSONS OF HOPE

this as a wrong number, Dini thought perhaps the lady had difficulty hearing, so she put the card aside and called the next day.

On day two, Dini called Manitoba and once again asked for Winnie. To her delight, the lady on the other end replied, "Yes, this is Winnie." Overjoyed, Dini tried to explain she had a card from Wilfred. Unfortunately, Winnie had limited hearing and the message was not transferring well. Dini began to speak slowly and as loud as she could. After nearly twenty minutes of Dini trying to explain who she was, and Winnie struggling to hear, Winnie suddenly said "Oh, Wilfred! Gail has been looking for Wilfred." Next, Dini asked who Gail was. Winnie offered up Gail's phone number. Dini eagerly scribbled it down. Unfortunately, Winnie offered a 12-digit phone number, two digits more than a typical North American phone number. We had no way to reach Gail. Dini called back.

On call three, it took some time for Winnie to remember who Dini was, but eventually, they got back on track. Dini tried to get Gail's surname, but Winnie didn't understand. Finally, when asking for Gail's phone number again, Winnie recited the ten digits we were looking for. Dini thanked Winnie and tried Gail's number, still unsure who Gail was. An answering machine clicked in, and Dini left a message explaining she had a card from Wilfred to deliver to Winnie.

The next day, I arrived at school around 7 AM. By the time I entered my office, I had three phone messages from Gail. I waited for Dini to arrive at school, and together we phoned Gail. Gail explained she was Wilfred's sister, and Winnie was their mom. Gail explained that Wilfred had been living

19

on the Downtown Eastside of Vancouver for quite some time. Wilfred would usually call once per year to let his family know he was okay, but this year they had not heard from him. Gail had left messages with the shelters, but she had no luck reaching Wilfred. She was delighted to learn that her brother was alive. She explained that two nights prior she had celebrated an early Christmas with her mom, Winnie, who was 94 years old. Winnie told Gail that she never cries about her husband who had passed away, as he lived a rich and fulfilling life, but every night, she cries for her son Wilfred, not knowing where he is, and whether or not he will be okay.

We couriered Wilfred's card to Winnie in Manitoba so she could have it on her bedside table, in time for Christmas.

### *A Mother-Daughter Reunion – Finding Noelle – Spring 2010*

Three days before Christmas, I found Noelle. She stood in the same place as the day we met. Noelle was overjoyed to hear we had found her daughter and grandchildren and that they wanted to see her.

Natalie let us know that she was saving money to fly to Vancouver to see her mom, but as a single mother of four, funds were tight. Again, my students knew it was time to take action. That spring, my students hosted evenings called 'Parents Night Out' where local families dropped off young children at our school while the parents enjoyed a night out. I ordered pizza for the kids and my students ran games and activities. The kids had a great time, and all funds raised were put towards our reunion plans. As Mother's Day approached, we had raised enough money to fly Natalie to Vancouver. A local hotel and some local businesses made donations. We were ready to surprise the women with a special mother-daughter reunion weekend.

We phoned Natalie the night before Mother's Day to let her know we would like to reunite her with her mom and pay all the expenses. Natalie was beside herself. She squealed with excitement and shouted, "WHO ARE YOU PEOPLE?"

On Mother's Day, two of my students joined me and we drove to find Noelle. She was not on her usual corner. We drove through the neighborhood, looking at the sea of people lost on Vancouver streets. We were about to give up when we spotted Noelle walking into an alley. I quickly parked the car and we headed in her direction, a laneway drenched in drug deals and poverty. Noelle leaned against the brick wall in an old white tank top and jeans. With less clothing, her tiny frame made it obvious she could not weigh more than 100 pounds. Noelle smiled when she saw us. We let her know we had a Mother's Day surprise, and that Natalie was coming to visit. Tears streamed down Noelle's face. We let her use my phone so she could hear her daughter's voice.

"Baby, it's Mom. I love you! I can't wait to see you!" Noelle was all smiles. As we walked away, an alley full of despair turned to an alley of joy as Noelle spread the news and others began to celebrate with her. Noelle's dream was coming true.

On a Wednesday in June of 2009, we picked up Noelle from her typical street corner and drove her to the Vancouver International Airport to pick up her baby girl. The moment was everything they had hoped. Within minutes, Noelle and Natalie were lost in conversation, making up for lost time. Their laughs were remarkably similar, as were their personalities. Natalie traveled with a thick photo album, allowing Noelle to catch up on their ten years apart. We checked Noelle and Natalie into their hotel room and I made plans to meet them for dinner the following evening.

On Thursday evening, my hairdresser and friend, Darci, joined me and met Noelle and Natalie at their hotel. Darci gave Natalie and Noelle free haircuts before dinner. As we hung out in the hotel room as friends, Noelle and Natalie reminisced about Natalie's childhood. They spoke of a kind and loving aunt who would have extended family over for holiday dinners even though she lived in a one-bedroom apartment. The cousins would all hang out together, jumping on the bed and laughing. It reminded me of my childhood, as I would spend hours and hours with my cousins at our grandparents' cabin. In fact, Noelle reminded me of my grandmother who I lovingly called Nanna. Both had Metis heritage, and both seemed to be the heart of their family. Darci and I shared stories of our childhoods, and it was easy to see that despite our differences, we had found common ground.

We headed to the *Boathouse Restaurant* along the ocean in English Bay. Noelle was mesmerized by the sights and sounds. Although we were only two miles away from the Downtown Eastside, we both knew the two neighborhoods were worlds apart. Natalie helped Noelle with her dinner. Life on the streets had impacted Noelle's teeth so Natalie took time to cut her mom's food into small pieces. It was the first time in over two decades that Noelle had sat down to enjoy steak, seafood and potatoes for dinner. She ate every bite.

After dinner, Noelle was exhausted, so Natalie walked her back to the hotel to allow her to get some rest. Darci and I lingered at the restaurant, savoring every moment of the evening. At least for one night, we were one, connected by shared experiences – all welcome in a restaurant, all eager to share childhood memories, and all grateful to have a place to go home to where we could curl up for a good night's sleep. We paused, knowing our common ground would only last for 48 hours. Once the reunion was over, Noelle would return to her harsh reality of life on the streets, and Natalie would fly back to Alberta.

When we arrived at the hotel, Noelle's tiny frame was curled up in a lush white comforter on the king-size bed. At least for this weekend, Noelle had escaped the never-ending sirens of the Downtown Eastside and stale smells of the homeless shelter. We said goodnight and excused ourselves as Noelle drifted off to sleep, side by side with her daughter, healing their broken connection.

*"No connection can ever be broken*
*if love holds tight at both ends."*
*Shannon L. Alder*

# SECTION

EVERYONE HAS A STORY

*"Be kind, for everyone you meet is fighting a hard battle."*
*Plato*

# Chapter 4
## Finding Light

*"If light is in your heart, you will find your way home."*
*Rumi*

### *Beyond HELLO – Spring 2013*

By 2013, *Project HELLO* had developed into a year-round initiative in three communities. Elementary-aged students in Coquitlam, Maple Ridge and Kelowna, BC were making handmade cards at Christmas and Mother's Day and high school students were heading to the streets to engage in conversation. We had made close to 500 connections, helping people reconnect through phone calls, greeting cards and face to face reunions. By all accounts, my idea was a success, but I had a growing sense that something was missing.

The men and women on the streets were trusting me with their stories. Word had spread. People were approaching us and asking for our help. Often, our students would have a short line of people waiting to send messages of love. In many instances, people would break down in tears after writing their first few lines. In a neighborhood based on raw survival, vulnerability was not always welcome or safe.

For those who had lost touch with family, and masked the pain with drugs or alcohol, it was hard to open up and speak from the heart. Our cards seemed to be the safest way for the homeless to reach out, as the fear of rejection was less significant than it would be with a phone call or face to face reunion. Despite this, something was still missing. People were speaking straight from the heart and wanting to share their stories. We were opening old wounds, but we were not responding with enough time or attention. If there was one thing we had learned, it was that everyone on the streets had a story worth hearing. I knew that the five-minute conversations we were having were not sufficient. I needed to go deeper.

I decided to go *Beyond HELLO*. I made the personal commitment to take a homeless person to lunch each month, inviting them to share their life story over a warm meal. I created www.BeyondHELLO.org as a space to share stories from the streets. When *Project HELLO* began five years earlier, my goal was to help the homeless experience the joy of giving. This time, with *Beyond HELLO,* my goal was to do more. My goal was to shift the perception of homelessness, one story at a time. I believe that when we understand one another's stories, judgment dissipates. With understanding, we are more likely to connect with compassion and begin to find solutions to heal a community.

Throughout the remaining chapters, I have woven stories from the streets with the lessons I have learned. To protect anonymity, names have been changed.

Cindy was the first person I met when I decided to go *Beyond HELLO*. Her story changed my life and taught me to believe in miracles. This chapter tells her story of courage and unwavering love.

### *All Too Familiar Streets – July 18, 2013*

It was time to go *Beyond HELLO*. The idea was simple. I would head to the Downtown Eastside and hand out water. I would start conversations, and then invite one homeless person to go for lunch. Over lunch, I would ask deeper questions to understand life on the streets. I invited David to join me. Five years prior, David had helped begin *Project HELLO* as a tenth grader, and now, he was home from university for the summer holidays. With two cases of water and some good intention, we headed to the streets.

David and I were both familiar with the streets of the Downtown Eastside as we had visited the neighborhood dozens of times with *Project HELLO*, so it caught us both off guard when we approached with trepidation, not knowing what to expect. How would we invite someone to lunch? How would we decide whom to choose? What would we say? We decided to load two backpacks full of bottled water and walk the streets. When the moment felt right for either of us, we would ask someone to join us for a meal.

After two blocks and brief encounters, we approached a lady who appeared in need. She stood alone on the street, with ragged clothing, and unkempt hair. When we offered her a bottle of water, she accepted but scolded us saying that what she needed was money for a meal as she was starving. She asked us how water was supposed to help. We replied by saying we were heading out for lunch and we would love for her to join us at a local diner, *Save-on-Meats*, if she was interested. She thought for a second and then accepted our invitation. Seeming somewhat ashamed to be with us, or ashamed she had accepted our offer, she walked ahead at a rapid pace. I asked her name, and she replied with one word—"Cindy."

We introduced ourselves, and for the next few minutes, we walked behind her, offering water to others as we made our way to the diner. Both David and I had the same feeling. We had selected the wrong person. She appeared somewhat erratic on the streets, crossing through intersections diagonally and attempting to ignore or avoid any small talk with us. Moving vehicles were flying towards her, and it didn't seem to faze her. The thought crossed my mind to offer Cindy money so she could eat elsewhere, and we could find someone else to join us.

As we entered the alcove of *Save-on-Meats*, things changed. Overcome with emotion, Cindy experienced a mental breakdown. She turned to us and frantically explained that she had no idea who we were or why we were there, but that she was highly suicidal. She feared for her life because of a drug debt and believed today was the day she would die by murder or suicide. In a rage of emotion, she frantically explained her suicidal ideation, continually telling us she had decided that today was the day. She could not understand why we had chosen to help her. She had made the decision to step in front of a city bus, but then we approached and asked if we could take her to lunch.

David and I helped Cindy with the door and asked the waitress for a table for three. We acknowledged the stress Cindy was under and motioned for her to come in and sit with us so we could try to help. Again, overcome with emotion, and with fear in her eyes, she flung herself into the booth and she began to open up.

Cindy admitted to us that she was an addict. She called herself a junkie, knowing her addiction controlled her. She shared that she was also HIV positive. Her extremities appeared swollen and inflamed, and her right leg was clearly infected. Her body was in septic shock. She knew she was very sick and that she should be in the hospital. She knew it was time for her leg to be amputated, but she was too scared to follow through. Hospitalized recently, she told us how she yanked her IV tubes out and escaped back to the Downtown Eastside so she could feed her addiction.

With tears in her eyes, she explained that she had cheated a friend to get her last hit of heroin. She owed the dealer $20, and if she did not pay, she feared her friend would be physically beaten. Looking in her eyes, I knew the fear was real. In our conversation, she fixated on suicide, explaining her urge to jump off a bridge or step in front of a bus. Although I never give money out on the DTES, something told me this was different, and that Cindy was telling us the truth. I heard myself say to Cindy that things would be okay. I decided to help take some of her stress away. I let her know I would give her $20 after lunch. Cindy started to relax but was still overcome with fear of what may happen. The waitress approached and Cindy ordered a Coke, a strawberry shake, a burger and fries. She then sheepishly asked if she could have the $20 right away, so she could go take care of the debt before lunch and relax knowing her friend's safety would no longer be in jeopardy. I heard myself agree and I handed Cindy $20. As David and I sat together in the booth, we quickly reflected, wondering if she would return. I asked David if he believed her story, and in complete agreement, he said, "Yes, you can see it in her eyes."

Five minutes later, Cindy returned. A weight had been lifted off her shoulders. With panic gone, we began to see the real Cindy, and we engaged in a great two-hour conversation.

Cindy was almost speechless, wondering why we had chosen her to take for lunch. David and I explained *Project HELLO* and the connections we had made through our card program. Through conversation, we realized that we had helped two of Cindy's friends find family members. We used David's phone to show Cindy pictures of her friends Rosemary and Noelle and told her about the connections we helped them make. She was in disbelief and again thanked us sincerely. She continued to explain that today was the day she had chosen to die. Right before we approached her, her thoughts were shouting out that no one in this entire world cared about her. Looking in our eyes with a calmness and softness that had not existed on the streets, she told us that she felt a higher power at work today as we were exactly what she needed. Through tears of appreciation, she told us that we seemed real and grounded. We thanked her for her words and explained to her that this was our first day of *Beyond HELLO* and she was the first person who seemed like they could use some company and a good meal.

As our food arrived, Cindy excused herself to wash her hands. Feeling like the food presentation was not appropriate for a suicidal woman, I removed the sharp knife that was projecting straight up from Cindy's burger. She returned with wet hands and embraced her burger and milkshake with childlike wonder. Although she had lived across the street for twenty years, this was the first time she had been in the restaurant, and the first time in years that she had ordered from a menu. Despite her appearance, the wait staff treated her with respect, and it seemed like Cindy was no different than anyone else in the diner.

Through lunch, I explained to Cindy how her story could inspire others. I acknowledged her heart and spirit. We could see the spark she had within her, and I knew her story would help others see beyond the stereotypes that plagued her neighborhood. Together we agreed that today was not her day to die. I don't know why she stood out to us on the streets, but I agreed with Cindy that we were meant to meet. I invited her to tell us her story and asked permission to share it so others could understand the people of the DTES and the circumstances of their lives. She looked at us with pride and disbelief, moved by the glimmer of hope that her story could make a difference. She was honored and willing to share.

Cindy moved to the DTES at the age of 16. She was born to a middle-class family in Ontario. Her mom was a hard-working woman who was extremely health conscious. Cindy paused for a moment to let me know I reminded her of her mom. I laughed and told her that I was in the middle of eating french-fries so I couldn't be a health nut. She laughed too and told me her mom liked french-fries as well but would only allow herself to have one. As I continued to eat my fries, she continued her story.

Cindy left home when her step-father started to abuse her. As a teen, she found herself in another abusive relationship with a boyfriend who beat her. When she discovered she was pregnant, she tried to move home. She was not welcome back. She wanted her daughter to have a life better than the one she could provide so she offered her up for adoption. She then moved to BC in search of a new life, hoping the change would erase her pain.

With complete certainty, Cindy looked up and told us she had always wanted to meet her daughter, but she would need to get clean first. Unfortunately, Cindy had been in and out of rehabilitation programs, and although she had completed rehab twice over the past decade, the lure of the drugs in the neighborhood always drew her back. Hope was not enough. In the early days, she worked the streets of Vancouver, caught in a vicious cycle of prostitution and addiction. Cindy paused to thank us. It had been a long time since someone had wanted to sit and talk with her.

Cindy told us about her living conditions in her government-funded building. Despite her attempt to keep her room tidy, she could not help but feel the walls were closing in as bugs swarmed her tiny apartment entering through the ventilation system. The smells of chemical fumes were overwhelming. The hallways had blood stains and splatters on the walls and door handles. Broken needles were prevalent. Cindy showed us her foot, extremely infected from the tip of a needle lodged within her skin. Her leg was red and purple, three times the size it should be and covered in a rash up to her knee. She walked with a limp because of the pain. Her body appeared to be shutting down, yet her emotional pain ran much deeper.

Cindy continued to reflect on her decision to offer her baby for adoption. We could see the shame she felt, yet the eternal love of a mother was also evident. With Cindy's health struggles, she feared she might not have long to live. Her dying wish was for her daughter to know how much she was loved. David and I wrote down her daughter's first name and date of birth and promised to do what we could. Unfortunately, Cindy did not know her daughter's last name.

As we finished lunch, Cindy began to cry. With scholarly wisdom, Cindy explained that her actions as an addict did not align with her moral fibre. She knew she had hurt people to feed her addiction and she felt ashamed as she also knew that underneath, she was a good person. Cindy spoke of her recent run from the hospital. She escaped to feed her addiction, but also because she did not feel mentally prepared to die. She sought a sense of peace before the end of life, and she knew she had yet to find that. She questioned whether or not that was a selfish pursuit, noting that she often thought of people in Auschwitz who died in Concentration Camps. If they were not given time to mentally prepare for death, why should she be afforded such a luxury? She wrestled with this thought, continuing to crave a sense of serenity.

As the waitress brought us the bill, Cindy seemed at peace. She asked to use the washroom and returned completely cleaned up. Her hair was wet from a quick wash and was swept off her face in a tidy ponytail. She had scrubbed her face and hands and mentioned washing her feet in the sink. With a new lightness of spirit, she told us she no longer felt alone, and she believed she was ready to go to the hospital. I asked if she would like an ambulance or if she would like a ride to St. Paul's Hospital. Cindy then paused and asked if she could ask us for one final request. We invited her to share.

"Can we please take a detour on the way to the hospital? Can we go for a drive so I can see the ocean?"

"Yes, I think that's a great idea. How about we drive through Stanley Park?"

"Oh, can we stop for a minute so I can put my feet in the ocean? And could you please take my picture there and share it with my family?"

"Yes. I think that's a wonderful idea. I think you are ready to do that."

As I paid the bill, Cindy excused herself for a smoke break outside. We joined her minutes later and pointed to my car two blocks away along Hastings, an all too familiar street for Cindy.

We approached my car and let Cindy know she could have the front seat. She mentioned her stomach was doing flips. Perhaps it was nerves, or perhaps it was the milkshake, coke, fries and burger digesting together in a system that usually got by with so much less. We stood outside my car and the sights and smells of Hastings surrounded us. Drawn by her addiction, Cindy looked at me with one hand on the car door and asked if she could please have $20 for one more hit or some T3s to stop the pain. I said no. Cindy then asked for $10, then $7 and then $5. She wanted her drugs before she left so she could self-administer them while at the hospital. I looked her in the eyes and told her I would not give her money to feed her addiction. The hospital staff had the medication she would need.

Caught in turmoil, Cindy became paralyzed. I told her I could take her to the ocean, or I could take her to the hospital, but I would not give her money. Our eyes met and we both felt the pain, knowing that the Cindy we got to know had surrendered to the addiction once again. Her need for one more hit was stronger than her willpower to escape. I heard myself say, "Cindy, I think it's time David and I should go." I knew by looking at her that she felt the shame of another broken relationship. David and I got in the car. We sat and waited for a minute in case she could find the strength. Knowing she was not ready, I drove away slowly. I looked up at my rear-view mirror to see the reflection of Cindy hunched over the parking meter. I knew it was an image that would be burned in my mind forever.

### Miraculous Moment – Cindy's Daughter is Found – July 19, 2013

Life is full of miracles. I'm not exactly sure why we chose Cindy from the crowded streets of the Downtown Eastside. She seemed to be the right person at the right moment. When we drove home after meeting Cindy, I questioned whether our trip had done more harm than good. We left Cindy behind; sick, drug-addicted and longing for money we were not willing to provide. We also left with a promise—a promise to try and find her daughter—a promise we hoped we could keep.

This was when miracles began to happen. Late that Wednesday night, I sat awake writing my first blog post about Cindy. I also searched Facebook until nearly 1 AM. Blurry eyed, I found a profile for a girl with the same first name (Paige) and same birthdate as Cindy's daughter. Since Cindy had given her daughter up for adoption, she did not know her daughter's surname. I sent a message to Paige and the waiting began. A couple of hours later, I realized the last Facebook status update on Paige's profile was posted months ago, so I felt discouraged, not knowing whether or not the message would be received through an inactive account. And then, at 3 AM, I had an idea. What if I randomly scrolled Paige's 'Friends' list on Facebook to find someone who could perhaps reach her? I scrolled past her first twenty friends, and then the first miracle took place. I saw the magic words "one mutual friend" under a man's photo. It turns out one of my past students, Aaron, went to university with a guy named Matt who went to grade school in Ontario with Cindy's daughter Paige. Talk about six degrees of separation!

By midday Thursday, Cindy's daughter Paige sent me a message, confirming her identity and wishing to connect with her mom. Overcome with joy, Paige and I began to email back and forth. I explained to Paige that it might be difficult to learn about her mom's lifestyle. Paige assured me she was ready, as she too had struggled with addiction.

I soon discovered Paige was a poet and an artist. Two years prior to our call, she requested her adoption papers in search of her mother. She had found out her mother's name and knew she had traveled to BC decades ago. Not knowing anything else about her mother, she began to write poetry about the topics of addiction and adoption.

Paige was convinced a particular book saved her life. She insisted I read it, as it was about Vancouver's Downtown Eastside. When Paige was struggling with addiction, she found solace in the book, *In the Realm of Hungry Ghosts,* written by Dr. Gabor Maté. The book tells the personal stories of Dr. Gabor Maté's patients, struggling with addiction on Vancouver's streets. One chapter, entitled

*Pregnancy Journals,* resonated so much with Paige that she credits her recovery to the book. She too, was pregnant, and she knew she had to get clean to keep her baby. The chapter, *Pregnancy Journals,* tells the story of a woman named Celia, who fought with her addiction in an attempt to keep her baby.

Paige was so moved by the book that she wrote to Dr. Maté to thank him for his work. I let Paige know that this was another strange coincidence. Dr. Maté and I share a mutual friend. When I began *Project HELLO* in 2009, he signed a copy of his book and thanked me for my work on the Downtown Eastside. It was a gift I treasured. I was eager to get back to the streets and find Cindy. I googled the phone number of the government-funded shelter that Cindy lived in and Dr. Gabor Maté's name popped up! Intrigued, I clicked the link only to discover that he had been the resident doctor with the organization supporting Cindy. Amazed, I wrote to Paige to let her know. We kept our fingers crossed that we would find Cindy again and make a connection.

### *Poetry & Plants – July 19, 2013*

David and I met at 10 AM that morning to drive downtown. With photos and Paige's poetry in hand, we were hopeful that we could find Cindy. We walked to her residence and met with the workers at the front desk. They were hesitant to get Cindy as her mental state can vary, and they didn't know if she could handle our news as she had been quite sick and unstable in recent days. They worried our news might trigger depression. I thought the opposite and wondered if our news could give her hope and inner peace. The worker knocked on her door but returned to say she did not answer and that she must be sleeping. We left our number, and they agreed to call us if they saw her. We agreed to stay in the neighborhood.

Approximately an hour later, we decided to move our car to a new meter and charge the phone for a couple of minutes. As we drove down Hastings, we saw Cindy dancing on a street corner. We quickly parked. Cindy looked at us. We looked at her. There was a pause where we were not sure if she was happy to see us. That changed in an instant. Cindy was in a great mood and busy selling plants. She had three beautiful potted plants; two lavender and one aloe plant that she was selling. I have no idea where they came from, but I was shocked at how many people who clearly did not live in this neighborhood were walking by asking, "How much?" Cindy told me the plants would sell for $5 each. I offered to buy two. For some reason I felt better buying plants than giving her cash, even though I knew where the money would go. However, I felt there was something symbolic about the plants and the connection we were about to make. The thought of watching a plant grow sat well with me.

I asked Cindy if she recalled our lunch meeting from two days ago. She looked at me like I was crazy and said, "Of course!" We then proceeded to tell her we had found her daughter. Cindy was shocked and overjoyed. She clenched both my hands with hers and tears flowed. At one point, I reached to support her as I thought she might faint. She read her daughter's poetry and listened as we told her everything we knew about Paige. When we told her that her daughter traveled to BC at a young age, she smiled and commented: "She has her mom's adventurous spirit."

Cindy hugged me tightly, clinging to the photos and began to celebrate by showing her friends pictures of her daughter. She asked us to walk with her to a corner store to show the shop owner. He offered to take a photo for us. I then asked Cindy if she had ever met Dr. Gabor Maté, and I let her know her daughter was impacted by his book. Cindy looked at me with what I first suspected was a blank stare and then said, "Do you mean Dr. Maté, the author of *In the Realm of Hungry Ghosts?*"

It was my time to stare. I nodded yes. Cindy was stunned. *Not only was Dr. Gabor Maté her doctor, she was a main character in the book, under the pseudonym Celia!* The chapter, *Pregnancy Journals,* that resonated with Paige in Ontario was all about Cindy and her attempt to keep her baby while battling addiction. *Paige had been reading about her own birth mother!* Cindy and I relished in disbelief, overcome with joy, love and gratitude, knowing we were experiencing a miracle together.

With life falling into place, Cindy was ready to go to the hospital and asked if we could take her. Armed with photos of her daughter, she had found the strength to get better. We asked if she was ready to call Paige. Cindy whispered, "Not quite yet. This is overwhelming. I'm not quite ready."

David asked Cindy what she planned to do with the third plant. Inspired by the events of today, Cindy asked us to join her at a community garden on the DTES so she could donate the plant and write a note to her daughter to leave beside it. She found an old paper plate and within minutes wrote a beautiful poem. She bent down close to the earth and used her hands to dig the soil and plant the lavender. Beside it, she left the photo we have given her from our lunch date, and a note:

*Donated by Cindy, July 19, 2013*

*To my daughter with love,*

*Spirits—seeds that bleed yesterday sorrow*

*In search of serenity in a new tomorrow*

Paige grew up across the country, not knowing her mother, yet both Paige and Cindy had turned to poetry to process emotion. I smiled at the uncanniness of their connection. David waited with Cindy on the street while I went to get the car. In the time that passed, 10-15 people purchased drugs off the street from an older lady who looked unassuming. Many were shooting up right there on the sidewalk. While waiting for the car, Cindy lifted up her pant leg, removed her Band-Aid, and injected her leg with heroin.

When I arrived with the car, Cindy got into the front seat and David hopped in the back. Again, Cindy requested we visit the ocean on the way to the hospital. She was elated and yelled goodbye to friends. She hugged the photos of her daughter. She asked if I had a smoke. I didn't. She yelled out my car window, and within a split second, while we waited at a red light, a lady ran to her passenger window. Cindy requested, "Canadian." The lady handed her a full pack of smokes. She turned to me and said, "I need five bucks." Again, not wanting to ruin the moment for Cindy, I paid for the cigarettes, and we started to drive towards Stanley Park to grant Cindy her wish of seeing the ocean.

It was 82 degrees in the city, traffic was thick, and the drive to Stanley Park took longer than expected, especially when Cindy realized we did not have a light. Regardless, she sat with her head out the car window marveling at the sights of Downtown Vancouver and the ocean only a few blocks away. She was mesmerized by the beauty. It had been more than twenty years since she had left the Downtown Eastside. Somehow, there seems to be an invisible fence keeping the poor confined to one area of Vancouver. Although Cindy lived blocks from the ocean, she did not feel free to wander from her impoverished street. We entered Stanley Park, and she almost jumped from the car when she saw a man smoking. I slowed down so she could get a light. She spotted the ocean but wanted me to keep driving to a beach area so she could put her feet in the sand. She couldn't wait to have her toes in the water and feel the healing waves of the ocean.

We parked the car at a beach area past Lumberman's Arch in Stanley Park. As I paid for parking, Cindy walked towards the water. We were on a grassy hill, looking down at the ocean. We were steps away from feeling the sand between our toes, and seconds away from calling Cindy's daughter, Paige, when suddenly things changed. The beauty and serenity of Stanley Park became insignificant as Cindy was hit with the sudden realization that she did not belong. Children splashed in the ocean and families pedaled by on bikes. Cindy stared out at a world she knew she was not part of. Frozen in her tracks, anger and rage took over.

Cindy yelled out to the world, "Life is not fair!" Tears fell as she shouted to the sky, "Get me out of these chains!"

Not knowing the best way to respond, I gave Cindy some time.

People stared as they passed us. We reassured them we were okay. David and I discussed whether we should call an ambulance. We asked Cindy. She made it clear she would not be getting in an ambulance. Cindy then told me she needed $20 fast to get her drugs. She felt completely overwhelmed, and the pain in her leg was excruciating. The sights of Stanley Park have shifted from mesmerizing to torturous. I explained to Cindy that I had no money left to give her and that no one around us was selling drugs. This did not sit well as Cindy was once again fixated on her next hit. She needed to get back.

We drove in silence. Every once in a while, Cindy turned and asked for money again. She claimed I must have $20— just not for her. Traffic was thick and it took time to crawl through the Downtown core. I was in the center lane. As we slowly approached Burrard Street, I tried to give Cindy a bit of a pep talk about her strength. I let her know that Burrard Street was approaching. It was time to make a decision. If I turned right, we would get to St. Paul's Hospital. If I turned left, I would get to Hastings and the Downtown Eastside. Without hesitation, she chose left. I let her know I would deliver the photos and poetry to the front desk of her shelter. I drove her home, parking along Hastings Street. Needing a hit, and still upset I was not providing cash, she took off from the car, taking my two plants with her so she would have something to sell to fund her addiction.

With my heart aching for Cindy's daughter Paige, I sent an email explaining our day. I shared the love and joy, the community garden, the poetry, and the trip to the ocean. I let her know I had photos I could send from the day. Unfortunately, Cindy had not found the peace she needed to make a phone call. Paige understood, but also ached knowing that contact with her mom was her missing puzzle piece. More than anything, she wanted to speak to her mom for the first time. She feared this might not happen. She needed the connection to heal her soul. With hope, I agreed to visit Cindy again soon, and together we prayed for the moment Cindy would be ready to reach out and make that first call.

Four days later, we headed back to the streets to see if Cindy might be ready to reach out and hear her daughter's voice. This is my blog post from that day.

### *Mom and Daughter Speak for the First Time – July 23, 2013*

While millions of people around the world waited in anticipation for the presentation of a royal baby, I was in search of another new beginning. For William and Kate and the royal watchers, July 23rd, 2013 was a significant day in history as it was the day Prince George of Cambridge was introduced to the world. A royal baby signified a new beginning and a new family bond.

In stark comparison, I too waited in anticipation. I walked the streets of Canada's darkest neighborhood, the Downtown Eastside of Vancouver, in hopes of finding Cindy. I crossed my fingers and hoped that it would be the day Cindy would be ready to reach out and hear her child's voice for the first time.

Our day began as a scavenger hunt. The streets were busier than usual, and behaviors seemed more extreme than normal. Even the familiar faces that normally welcome us to the neighborhood seemed a little less cheerful – probably a combination of the hot weather, the full moon and the monthly payday still two long days away. David and I walked the streets for an hour hoping to find Cindy. We decided to see if she was at the homeless shelter. We took the elevator up to her floor of the government-funded building. The elevator itself seemed more like a crate, with nothing but stained metal sides and cracked buttons. Through the narrow halls, we found her door with a memo stuck to it, requesting she bag her clothes so they could spray for bed bugs. We knocked and waited. No answer.

Back on the streets, we walked up and down the hot pavement. We spoke with those who looked curious, showing a photo of Cindy, and asking if they had seen her. Most had. Cindy was well known in the DTES as she had survived the streets for over twenty years. Despite her temper and drastic mood swings, Cindy was well liked. She was intelligent, articulate, creative and passionate. Despite her traumatic life story, she was a strong woman. When she opened up, and made sincere eye contact, others could see her soul buried under layers and layers of hurt. She had a tough life and was her own worst enemy, yet underneath, a woman existed with moral values and a big heart. As we spoke to others on the street, they each had something positive to say about Cindy. One woman, named Lilly, told us about her journey through detox with Cindy. Fortunately for this woman, she had managed to stay clean. She suggested we try *InSite*, the safe injection site (a facility designed to prevent the spread of disease and overdose by offering clean needles and medically supervised injections).

As we entered *InSite*, we were caught up in a steady stream of clients trying to enter the building through a narrow entrance ramp. Others leaving shuffled their way through the narrow path, bumping into one another in the tight space. Some brought their bikes in with them as there was no security in leaving them unattended on East Hastings Street.

The staff were busy checking clients in and out, so we stepped aside to the waiting area until they had a moment. The staff at *InSite* were wonderful, nurturing and respectful, and spent time listening to us about our project. They could not release confidential information, but they told us that they would be happy to help by passing on information to Cindy. We left a note with them, including Paige's phone number and then made our way back to the streets.

In our last attempt before heading to the car, we saw Cindy a few steps away from *InSite*, standing in front of the community garden where she planted the lavender for her daughter days before. Cindy looked alive and vibrant. She was wearing jeans, a red tank top and a grey headband. She almost looked stylish—a drastic comparison to her outfits the week before.

David and I approached Cindy again, not knowing whether she would welcome our visit. This time she did. She started by saying she could not believe our timing as she was just thinking about us. I told her that I had more news about her daughter. I let her know that her daughter had shared more poetry and we had printed it for her. I also let her know that her daughter had lived a life with some similar struggles. She too had a baby at sixteen, and she had also struggled with addiction.

Cindy realized this meant she was a grandma! I let her know her granddaughter's name and tears of love poured down her face. Her legs became weak, and she had to hold on to me for stability. The news was so powerful that she needed to sit. Beside her, on the dirty streets, she had an overstuffed brown teddy bear. She used the bear as her pillow and sat down. Cindy stared deeply into my eyes not wanting to miss a single word as I told her about my emails back and forth with Paige. I assured her that her daughter understood her and let her know that her daughter would love to say hi. Cindy looked to me for strength and said okay. I called the number and listened to the rings at the other end. After three rings, I began to worry that we would not make a connection. Then, I heard the voice of her daughter on the other end. I let Paige know that Cindy was ready to say hello.

Cindy took my phone and whispered, "Hi baby. It's your mom." Tears fell as she reached out and held my hand. She squeezed tightly as I encouraged her to keep going, rubbing her back while she spoke. The first thing she asked her daughter was whether or not the adoption agency had given her the six-page letter she had left explaining all the reasons she had to offer her up for adoption. They had not. Like a woman on a mission, Cindy condensed the six pages into a three-minute explanation about her teenage years, her abusive boyfriend, her lack of support and her most difficult decision. Paige understood.

The conversation became a bit lighter and the two of them discussed pottery and poetry. Both women have an artistic, creative spirit, and felt the connection with one another. Cindy then listened as her daughter spoke. While I did not hear what her daughter said, I know it was heartfelt as Cindy's emotion was one I cannot even describe. All I can say is that her face was overcome with expressions I have only witnessed through media after a tragedy has occurred. With a mix of love, anguish and grief, her mouth seemed to stretch back, and her eyes focused intently as tears poured from her face. It was the rawest emotion I have ever experienced. I cannot find the words to describe it well but know I will never forget this image.

Overcome by her emotion, Cindy tilted her head back and let the phone fall gently from her hand to the sidewalk. I picked up the phone to see how Paige was doing. I asked Cindy if she had anything else to say. Through grief, she asked me to tell her she loved her. I told her she had the courage to say it herself and held the phone to her ear while she whispered to her daughter that she loved her. It was a conversation Cindy had dreamed about for over twenty years, yet finding family when life is limited seemed so unfair. With a mix of shame and hope, love and pain, Cindy handed the phone back to me and let her head fall gently back on the sidewalk against the teddy bear. I let her daughter know I would be in touch soon, and we hung up.

We sat with Cindy as she cried, staining her daughter's poetry in fresh tears. For the first time in Cindy's life, she had heard her baby speak. She heard forgiveness for her most difficult decisions. She heard acceptance despite her lifestyle. Through loving words, a mother-daughter connection was made, helping both of their souls heal. Their missing puzzle piece had been found. For Cindy, it was bittersweet. She had waited her whole life to feel the unconditional love that exists between a parent and a child and had now found it near the end of her life.

Together we sat hand in hand on the hard, stained pavement surrounded by graffiti and the smell of drugs. Together, despite our surroundings, we connected with compassion— all because these women had the courage to go *Beyond HELLO*.

### *The Missing Puzzle Piece – Plans to Connect – April 2014*

As summer came to an end, Paige made a promise to save money with the hopes of one day travelling to BC. By early May, she met her goal and found the money to take the trip. A friend in BC had invited her to stay free of charge for two weeks.

When Paige and I reconnected that spring, we both wondered if Cindy was still alive. We hoped Cindy's battle with HIV had not ended and that she would still be willing to meet. Paige left a message at Cindy's shelter, hoping she would call. After a couple of days, Cindy phoned Paige all on her own. The two shared stories, shed tears together and dreamt of a face to face reunion. Paige promised to book tickets soon. Cindy made a promise too. For the first time in two decades, she was ready to be free from addiction for good. She did not want her daughter to see her as an addict, so as Paige made travel arrangements, Cindy checked herself into a treatment facility so she could be clean for their reunion. Throughout treatment, Cindy's nurse updated me with her commitment and progress. The nurse let me know that Cindy would complete rehab two days after Paige's arrival in Vancouver.

Paige arrived in Vancouver on a Thursday morning. On Saturday, Cindy called me. I will never forget the call. She thanked me from the bottom of her heart, told me with pride that she was clean, and arranged details for us all to meet on Monday. As we were about to hang up, she asked me to wait… she had more to say…. She wanted to make sure I would stay with her during the reunion so she could have support. She was nervous, and she needed friendship. I promised I would stay and let her know that it would be one of the best days of my life too.

I reached out to Dr. Gabor Maté to let him know the connection would happen that week. I asked if he could sign Paige's copy of *In the Realm of Hungry Ghosts*. He offered more. In a gesture of love, he reached out to Paige and invited her to his home for a two-hour visit. On Sunday morning, he inspired Paige with knowledge of her mother, the latest research around ADHD, parenting and addiction. He signed her book and wished her good luck with the reunion. He gave Paige the encouragement she needed to meet her mom face to face.

On Monday morning, I picked up Paige and headed to the DTES. Mother and daughter were about to meet. As we stood outside the treatment facility (our agreed meeting place), there was no sign of Cindy. Cindy had called to confirm earlier and had let me know she had invited her boyfriend Ron to join us. We stood and waited.

Minutes later, through the crowded sidewalk, I saw the smile I fell in love with months earlier. Cindy beamed as she approached, hand in hand with her boyfriend, Ron. Her hair was cut short, she was well put together in a nice pink sweater, and she swung a white shopping bag. She had stopped at the store to pick up three t-shirts and a pack of decorated hair barrettes for her daughter.

Time seemed to hit fast forward, and all of a sudden, the twenty-seven-year gap was over. Cindy and Paige embraced each other and recognized themselves in each other's smiles and sparkling eyes. While both ladies had asked me to help with the reunion, no help was needed. These two were meant to find one another. They found their other half. Without knowing one another, they had so much in common (poetry, art, struggles with addiction, a love for reading and writing, a habit of continually tapping their right leg, and more) Paige had found her missing puzzle piece.

Cindy presented Paige with a handwritten letter:

*My Dear Daughter,*

*It has been a long journey to get to where we are. We are only just beginning, and I hope and pray that we will get to have the friendship that my addiction took from my mother and me. One day at a time. Sweet Jesus. All my love, forever.*

*Your biological mother,*

*Cindy*

Ten months prior, I sat in *Save-on-Meats* diner, listening to Cindy's life story and her heartbreak of not knowing her daughter. Now, sitting in the same diner, I witnessed a miracle take place. Cindy, Paige and Ron connected as family with heart, compassion and understanding. They shared stories, caught up through photos, exchanged gifts and made plans to spend lots of time together over the next two weeks. They all agreed they wanted to share their story with the public, inspiring other families to reconnect and to understand addiction. Although I was there for support, the bond created was so strong that I knew in my heart this mother-daughter connection was unbreakable. I drove home, knowing that every one of us felt complete. We had found what we were looking for. Together, we found light on Vancouver's darkest street.

*"Darkness cannot drive out darkness: only light can do that. Hate cannot drive out hate: only love can do that."*
*Martin Luther King, Jr.*

# Chapter 5
## Good Vibes Only

*"Become friends with people who aren't your age.*
*Hang out with people whose first language isn't the same*
*as yours. Get to know someone who doesn't come from*
*your social class. This is how you see the world. This is*
*how you grow." Anonymous*

### Unexpected Happiness

I did not expect to find happiness on the Downtown Eastside of Vancouver. When I began *Project HELLO* and *Beyond HELLO*, I wanted to help make others happy. I didn't anticipate how much I would gain from the stories of those on the streets. Ironically, there is a wisdom that comes from those who have lost everything. While I have heard stories of heartbreak, I have also heard stories of resilience, courage and hope. My friends from Vancouver's streets have taught me that happiness does not come from what happens to you; it comes from how you choose to respond to what happens. Their stories ground me and remind me what matters.

The stories in this chapter demonstrate the power of the human spirit and the opportunity we have to find happiness, even in darkness. Chloe, Clay, Rhonda, Steve and Lee may be homeless, but that doesn't stop them from appreciating the little things in life.

### Sweet as Caramel – Lunch with Chloe – March 27, 2016

The thick caramel sauce dripped in slow motion from Chloe's sundae spoon as she told her story. The growing puddle on the table seemed irrelevant in comparison to her words, and the look in her eyes made it clear that the memory she was replaying was far more vivid than anything in front of us.

Twenty minutes before this, Chloe was out for her weekly walk through the Downtown Eastside Sunday Market, a cornered off street, crammed with vendors selling a range of items: old clothing, cigarettes, fresh and not so fresh foods and a collection of used and stolen goods. Aisles were crowded with the homeless population of Vancouver all out for a day of trade. Amongst the buying and selling, security evicted vendors unwilling to pay the one-dollar rental charge. The expression of most market-goers suggested purpose—a day about survival and profit. Chloe seemed different. Small in stature, and dressed in a mini skirt, nylons and bright blue clogs, she shivered under her white jacket. With her hood pulled over her head, she clenched a small bag of belongings and looked at displays with polite interest. Her kindness and mild manner caught my attention, so I suggested to Jas, a grade ten student, that we approach and offer Chloe the opportunity to sit down and have lunch. I tapped Chloe on the shoulder and explained that we were going for lunch and would love for her to join us. "Me? You choose me to ask? No one buys me lunch. Umm, sure. Why not? Yes, okay. I would love to come." After exchanging names, we were on our way to my favorite restaurant in the DTES, *Save-on-Meats*, a place where everyone is accepted and treated with a warm welcome.

Chloe showed interest in us and was pleasantly surprised that we would drive all the way downtown just to ask someone to go for lunch. I explained *Beyond HELLO* and our desire to help in a different way. Chloe loved that Jas was a student and asked lots of questions about high school these days. She mentioned she had moved many times in her life commenting, "Now that's how I got an education!" I agreed that each new experience offers authentic learning.

We invited Chloe to order anything she wanted from the menu. She loved the idea of a great big dessert followed by a grilled cheese. I told her I loved the way she planned her food around the dessert. When the waitress asked if she would like her dessert after her grilled cheese sandwich, she shook her head 'no' with slight bewilderment, "Why on earth would I want to wait for a great big ice cream sundae?" Good question—and one that those of us living with enough to eat don't have to ponder.

So, what brought Chloe to the DTES of Vancouver? I started by asking how long she had lived in the neighborhood. Like many, her dates were foggy, but she believed she had been in the DTES for 20 years. Chloe told us she was 47 years old. Minutes later, she corrected herself and said she had no idea how old she was—she celebrates the day but doesn't count the years. She was born in Poland in 1968. By most accounts, her family was successful. Her dad was an engineer, her mother worked in an office and they owned a condo and two cars. At age eleven, her dad accepted a job in Athens, Greece. It was supposed to be short term. Days after his departure, Chloe was hospitalized with abdominal pain. It should have been a simple three-day hospital stay at most. Instead, following an appendix removal, Chloe was infected by needles at the hospital, and she progressively got worse. Three months later, swollen yet skinny, her life expectancy was questionable. Her mom decided the treatment wasn't working and took her from the hospital and traveled to Greece to see Chloe's father. Chloe felt as if she was starving. With not much to lose in her dire condition, her mother let her eat whatever she felt like. She remembers eating grapes, chocolate, yogurt, cola and an occasional taste of her parent's alcohol. She stopped taking all her medication. Bit by bit, her health improved. With political unrest in Poland in 1980, her family lost their possessions and was not able to return home.

In her teen years, Chloe's family immigrated to Edmonton. Chloe recalls the nine-month winters and three-month summers. She has few happy memories as an only child in Edmonton and loved learning they would soon move to Vancouver.

The worst was yet to come for Chloe. Chloe paused to tell us she hadn't talked about this much before. She asked if Jas and I had ever had an experience that we knew was real but seemed like a nightmare because it was too horrible to comprehend. Losing interest in her sundae and staring straight ahead, she told us the details of a day in her 20's where she was in the shower and heard an altercation in the living room. The words and sounds didn't make sense. She knew it was her father's voice, but it was a side of him she had not seen or heard before. She found her mom dead in the living room. Paramedics tried to revive her without success. To this day, Chloe doesn't understand why her dad wasn't charged. No one interviewed Chloe about what happened. What was ruled a natural death was anything but natural for Chloe. She continued to share a residence with her father for one more month until he tried to strangle her. This was the tipping point, where homelessness became the more desirable option.

For two decades, Chloe has lived in the DTES. She has been drugged, robbed, sexually and physically assaulted. She relives her trauma when she sleeps. Despite the adversity she has faced, she finds beauty in simple things: a few close friends, the sunshine and the beauty of the city. She is not jaded. She finds good in people. The DTES community is her home, and it's where she feels accepted. The gentrification of the neighborhood bothers her. She is not upset with the development, but she is frustrated with elitist attitudes of new occupants. As Chloe says, she has traveled, she has been new to a city, and she believes we are all equal. No one is better than another person. She has no tolerance for racism or prejudice. She believes we are meant to coexist and form community. She looked at Jas and me and said, *"Our hearts are the same. It's only in our heads that we are different."* I asked if we could stop, so I could write down her quote as I couldn't agree more. She smiled and blushed as we complimented her on her wisdom.

After offering us her fries and engaging in conversation about all our families, Chloe requested a take-out box for her leftover food. I asked where she thought she would be in ten years. "Oh, probably right here, unless I'm dead. Some days I contemplate suicide, but nah—I don't think I'll do that. Life's too good for that."

## *Twisted Tranquility – Clay's Story – March 18, 2015*

Meet Clay. Like the complexity of Hastings Street, he is a mix of darkness and light. Scarred by the trauma of war, he now fights an inner battle of self-acceptance. He grew up in Saskatchewan, the youngest of three boys. His dad died at age 10. School was a struggle, and the military provided the guidance and structure he needed. However, nothing could have prepared him for war in Afghanistan. Ten years later, he cannot erase the images: families with young children living in caves, eleven-year-old war soldiers and friends lost in combat. The desire to help and protect his closest friends gave him the courage to return to war two times, fighting for our country.

Like so many veterans of war, Clay faced a silent battle after returning home. Anger. Confusion. Nightmares. Difficulty fitting in. Loneliness. Struggling with emotion, his anger got the best of him. His own mother feared him, his personal relationships deteriorated, and eventually, he spent time in a psychiatric ward where he was convinced all other patients were snipers. Eventually, the delusions subsided, but the pain remained.

Looking for a new life, Clay tried a variety of jobs in Vancouver: construction, moving furniture, living on a berry field, and raising and selling Rottweilers. He fell in and out of homelessness—not for lack of skill, but more from a lack of purpose. Now on disability, Clay is unable to work, and unfortunately unable to find housing. He tried living in BC Housing's SRO shelters, but the living conditions made the streets look favorable. The SRO housing was rough, with a neighbor who stole from him continually, and sanitary conditions that he refused to share in fear he would ruin our lunch together. One evening Clay's anger got the best of him. He won the physical fight with the neighbor but faced eviction as a consequence. He tried temporary shelters, but he couldn't keep his possessions safe while he slept, so instead, he took cover in Vancouver's back alleys.

Clay is grateful for a new best friend as the streets are safer in pairs. Together they share an alcove that they have declared theirs, and they take turns guarding each other's possessions. Their loyalty is strong and key for survival. Clay and his friend share a sense of enthusiasm and childlike wonder. As we met them in the middle of Pigeon Park (a street corner plagued by homelessness and home to hundreds of pigeons), they were playfully shooting a bow and arrow through the courtyard.

Beyond Clay's dark side, there is so much good within. He describes his mother as his best friend and speaks of one day moving back to Saskatchewan to be closer to her. He marvels at his 20-year-old daughter's beauty and brains. He shared her name, and together we found her on Facebook and scrolled through beautiful photos. I asked if he would like to send a message. He smiled and said he didn't need to—he was in touch. He also considered moving to Alberta to be closer to his daughter.

After Afghanistan, Clay knows the value of each day. He is frustrated by those around him who take life for granted. He recognizes that he is living in one of the most beautiful cities in the world, and each day is a blessing. After being homeless in most major cities in Canada, he describes Vancouver as the kindest. One day a family gave him a new coat. As they drove away, the son yelled, "Check the pockets!" He did—and found a twenty-dollar bill in each pocket—for a total of $100. He also spoke of a wealthy man in Vancouver who periodically brings a limo to the DTES and hands fifty-dollar bills out the window. For Clay, moments like that matter. Contrarily, he is completely offended (as am I) by the growing number of tour companies that include Hastings Street as a tourist attraction on their city bus tours.

There is an irony to Clay that I like. He's the first person I have taken to lunch who uses the word 'homeless' to describe himself, yet he might be the strongest person I have met. He spoke of the neighborhood as home for now, but he doesn't see it in his future. When I asked where he would be in five years, he answered, "A long way from here." Unlike others, Clay described the neighborhood like he was analyzing it from the outside looking in. He opened up more than most and explained the ins and outs of the neighborhood to us—the difference between each block; where each type of drug is sold; the gang activity and boundaries; the way debts are paid; and the unwritten code of conduct that treats men, women and children differently on the same streets. I shared my experience of feeling more accepted into the neighborhood when I am with other women versus men, and he instantly confirmed, "Yes, that's much safer. We all watch out for the women and defend them if they are in trouble." He also spoke about the rule to call out "Kids on the Block" each time kids are nearby (something I have heard numerous times). Even those in an addicted state want to do what they can to protect the innocence of children.

What keeps a man like Clay on the streets? Like most stories of the Downtown Eastside, the answers are much deeper than we assume. For Clay, it's not the poverty or addiction that keeps him there. I suspect it's the inner battle of acceptance and a struggle to renew his sense of worth. The Downtown Eastside offers a twisted tranquility to lost souls, an escape from reality and solace where everyone fits in. As Clay said goodbye, he left with intention—a plan to walk up to *Carnegie Center* to call his mom and his daughter. Maybe one day, when the time is right, he will return to his family.

### *Love on a Cold Street: 831 – Lunch with Rhonda and Steve – November 13, 2016*

On this autumn afternoon, Jenna and I headed to the Downtown Eastside to take someone for lunch. For me, the DTES of Vancouver is like therapy. It's a bold reminder of everything I should be grateful for, a wake up to what matters, and it's where time stops. There is no rush, no to-do list, and an appetite for authentic conversation exists.

Picking a guest for lunch is always an interesting process. People always ask how I choose, and my answer is always the same. I don't. They choose me. As Jenna and I walked the rainy streets of Vancouver and said hello to our city's most marginalized citizens, it was Rhonda who reached out to help us. Looking a bit out of place in our warm jackets and fall boots, Rhonda noticed us as guests to her neighborhood and asked if she could help:

"Hey, you guys looking for something?"

"Yes, we are heading out for lunch and looking to see if anyone on the streets would like to join us."

Thinking of others first, she turned to her two friends Mike and Steve and offered the meal to them. Mike was the first to accept. As we were about to head to the restaurant, Steve mentioned it was his birthday week, so why not indulge in a nice lunch. After a second thought, Rhonda decided she would join us too. Mike decided not to wait for a table and headed on his way, but Steve and Rhonda were happy to be inside the warm restaurant and eager to share stories. They asked if I was Jenna's mom. When she replied that I was her vice-principal when she was in high school, they both laughed. "A principal? Oh god."

I smiled, "Don't worry, I'm not that type." They laughed with a smile, suggesting they did not have positive memories of school.

As we sat down to lunch, Steve beamed. "I am the luckiest guy in the world." He asked if he could explain his philosophy of life. Of course, I agreed.

*I am the luckiest guy in the world. The world revolves around love. If you want love to grow, you have to give love. Our happiness is a choice: It's a decision we get to make. I live in a corner suite at ground zero. How could I be happier? I stand on the streets and get 600 hellos a day. Where else can you find that? I am 69, but I feel young, so I stay young. I really am the luckiest guy in the world. I get to wander these streets and help others realize they too have reasons to smile.*

Rhonda was equally positive. At first glance, her thick eyeliner, leather jacket, and tattoo suggested a hard edge. Rhonda asked if we understood the tattoo on her neck—three thick, black numbers: 8 3 1. We did not. She began to explain.

"Eight Letters. Three words. One meaning. It is code for *I Love You.*"

Rhonda and Tom share a similar philosophy, choosing to see the positives in an otherwise dark neighborhood. As we ordered lunch, Rhonda and Steve continued to banter back and forth with a friendly father/daughter-like relationship. Roommates for the second time in Vancouver's SRO housing, they have much to disagree on. He likes rock, she prefers rap. He likes sports, she prefers the arts. He is 69. She is 47. What unites them is their optimism, hope and happiness in a dark neighborhood. Both ex-convicts, they have experienced much, but now have a different philosophy on life. They now find happiness by helping others. Rhonda raved about her three sons living in Alberta and Ontario— all with artistic talents. Steve spoke fondly of his sister who is coming to visit from her small interior BC town. He may go back and stay with her for a few weeks. He may even stay for Christmas. But the town only has one street, one traffic light and no one lining the roads to offer him his 600 daily hellos.

The kindness and community of the Downtown Eastside is where these two find what we all look for: a place to love, a place to be loved and a place to belong.

### *Feeling Alive – Lunch with Lee – October 26, 2013*

At 66 years old, Lee has defied the odds. On the Downtown Eastside of Vancouver, those who make it to the age of 40 are considered seniors and eligible for discount cards. Yet, as Lee told us, he doesn't feel old. With sparkling eyes and a youthful spirit, he feels alive. Lee has survived the dark days on East Hastings and has lived to tell about it. He has learned some hard lessons in life and paid the price, serving time behind bars a few years ago for drug trafficking. He doesn't make excuses. He admits he was on the wrong path, and prison was what he needed to never go back to old habits. He lives without regret, and wouldn't change his past, as it has shaped who he is today. With a toothless smile and laugh lines in all the right places, Lee demonstrates an admirable sense of resilience. Living in Canada's poorest neighborhood has not dampened his spirit.

In month four of *Beyond HELLO*, Lee joined my principal Sean and me for a late lunch, agreeing to share his story in exchange for a warm meal. Lee reflected on his life with an appreciation for the good times, even finding the positive lessons that emerged from his time behind bars.

Lee grew up in a Chinese immigrant family, attending local Vancouver schools. He never exceled at school, and at the age of 18, he had only achieved a grade eight education. With a need for adventure and a curious spirit, Lee joined the army. In his four years of service, he traveled the world, serving our country. His favorite adventures include the warm Mediterranean water in Cyprus and training days jumping from planes at the Army Airborne School in Alberta.

After four years of service, Lee returned to BC and took a job in Prince George. Initially, he worked in a kitchen and shortly after, he took a physical job at the mill. He hated the manual labor of the mill and decided to explore his love of the kitchen. Lee reminisced about days working at some of the top restaurants in town. He worked his way up from kitchen help to 2$^{nd}$ cook and eventually to head cook. The hours were long, the lifestyle was draining, and the split shifts consumed all of his time. Facing exhaustion, he decided to make a change and venture to Toronto to live near his brother. It was in Toronto that he found the balance he was looking for.

He fell in love, married his wife, and secured a job as a baker for *Loblaws*, a job he kept for over two decades. Unlike most I have talked to, Lee does not seem angry about his past. He does not blame anyone but himself. He let us know his marriage fell apart, his brother died, his parents died, and he had turned to drug trafficking as his means for survival. The streets of Vancouver became his home. Unlike most whose eyes search for approval or understanding when sharing their story, Lee is different. He is accepting of his mistakes and seems to have forgiven himself for the pain he has caused others. Perhaps this is why Lee has survived to 66 in Canada's roughest neighborhood. His lightness is perhaps his best survival skill.

Today Lee lives month to month, relying on his old age security checks. He lives in modest, low-income housing, yet he takes pride in his home, where he has his own kitchen, his own television and space for his roommate, Scarlett, the cat.

Through our conversation, we took some time to tell Lee a little about our lives. When we mentioned we were high school administrators, he smiled back at us saying, "That's okay," with an understanding that many who have failed at school do not have the fondest memories of the principal's office. Lee was surprised that we had driven from Maple Ridge to take someone for lunch. I let him know a little about *Beyond HELLO*, sharing my goal of taking one person to lunch each month. I explained my view that the neighborhood is plagued by unnecessary judgment and that each person on the streets has a story worth hearing. He smiled in agreement.

When I asked Lee what he would want others to know, he paused momentarily and then explained how the neighborhood works: "Everyone knows everyone. We may not know all the names, but we know the faces. It is a community, yet everyone living on the streets has their own means for survival."

I suspect Lee's positive disposition may be his strongest assct. His smile spread ear to ear when he told us that even the police who walk the streets of Hastings enjoy him now because they know he is drug-free and only sells cigarettes for extra income.

Knowing that Lee could recognize most faces of the DTES, I decided to ask him if he knew some of the people I had connected with. I asked him if he knew Noelle, otherwise known as 'Little Momma.' I described her in detail, as the first woman I had met on the DTES back in 2009. I spoke of her slender build, her mobility struggles, and her kind heart. Within seconds, Lee knew exactly who I was talking about, and with excitement, as if he had big news to share, he blurted out rather loudly, "Hey, did you know she found her daughter?" With equal excitement, and perhaps less humility, I blurted back, "*I* found her daughter!"

Finding Noelle's daughter Natalie was the springboard for *Project HELLO* and the inspiration for my students and me to turn our one-day field trip into a lifelong project. To have someone living on the Downtown Eastside quote this story back to me *almost four years later*, someone who had no idea that I had anything to do with the reunion in the first place, was magical.

In a simple second, something changed. Lee knew he had made my day, just as much as I had made his. After paying the bill, we ventured back out to Hastings in hopes of touching base with Noelle. With a genuine eagerness to help, Lee called out behind us, "I hope you find her." The sound of his voice said more than his words. In the time it took to eat a meal, Lee had experienced another significant moment in a life worth living; another reason to smile and feel alive.

*"Through adversity to the stars!" Royal Air Force*

# Chapter 6
## The Grace of a Woman

*"I will hold myself to a standard of grace, not perfection."*
*Emily Ley*

### Thanks Mom

I grew up surrounded by strong women. My grandma was an emergency room nurse and my mom was a teacher, and later, a school principal. For generations, the women in my family have been hardworking, compassionate, and connected to their community. Despite busy schedules, family always comes first.

My mom doesn't let things get to her. When I was little, she would always tell me, "There is no such thing as a problem—only creative solutions." My mom thinks so far outside the box that sometimes she forgets the box exists. I'll give you an example. Last year my mom had an appointment at the bank. The appointment was supposed to be short, so she wasn't too worried about the frozen groceries in her trunk. When she arrived at the bank, the receptionist apologized and said it would be a twenty-minute wait. Instead of rescheduling, or waiting and worrying about the defrosting groceries, my mom did not miss a beat.

"No problem," she replied. "Do you have a freezer in your staff room?"

"Yes?" the reception answered inquisitively.

"Great. Grab your jacket. We will head down to my car together and load my groceries upstairs and into your freezer. That way, I won't worry about my groceries defrosting, and I can wait for the appointment!"

Stunned, the receptionist grabbed her coat and helped my mom load the frozen foods into the bank's staff room freezer. The irony is my mom doesn't see this as creative or outside the box. It's who she is. She is 100% authentic and says and does whatever she likes.

My mom never complained about being a single mom. In fact, she made it look easy. Somehow, she balanced two kids and a full-time job in education, while also owning a catering company that catered weddings and special events in the evenings or on weekends. My mom has always had a way of holding it together.

The women on the streets demonstrate a similar type of resilience. Their stories inspire me, as they model courage, compassion, empathy and grace. Every single woman I have met on the Downtown Eastside has been sexually and physically assaulted. Despite their dire circumstances, they still manage to rise from adversity and nurture others in the neighborhood. The women look out for one another and keep each other safe, almost instinctively.

### Safety on the Streets – May 2019

In May of 2019, I was on the streets with two students inviting people to write Mother's Day cards. As we walked up the street, I could hear commotion behind me and noticed a man walking barefoot and shirtless. He appeared to be in a drug-induced rage of excited delirium. He shouted at everyone he passed, threatening many as he forced his way up the street.

I instantly felt unsafe – a feeling I don't usually experience even on the Downtown Eastside. A police officer drove by, and I almost flagged him down, but then I felt foolish, knowing my fear was only a gut feeling. Nothing had happened to me. As the man caught up to us, we stayed silent, hoping he would carry on. Instead, he decided to walk directly beside me. He began to harass us, and I politely asked him to give us space as I was with students. He ignored my request. The students and I turned off Hastings Street, hoping our side street would deter him. No such luck. He proceeded to walk right behind me as if to intimidate me. My credit card was in my back pocket, so I felt uneasy having someone travel so close. I motioned for the students to help a homeless lady crouched over in a doorway to our right. They approached with Mother's Day cards and began to help her reach out to her mother. I turned to the man behind me and told him he was making me feel uncomfortable.

He grabbed hold of my arm and mocked me, "You don't feel comfortable? How do you think I feel?" He held my arm with a firm grip, and I froze for a second, not sure what to do next. Without hesitation, I heard the woman from the doorway yell, "Here—take my drugs. Take it all!" She opened her pockets and gave him everything she had. He released my arm, happy to victimize someone else, and ran up the street. The woman sitting in the doorway smiled at me and apologized, "Sorry about that. What a jerk. I don't even know him." She may not have known him, but she knew how to survive on the streets and how to keep me safe.

I have visited the Downtown Eastside hundreds of times. Only twice have I felt unsafe. I wish I knew the lady's name who gave away her drugs to protect me. I wish I had offered more than a simple thank you. In a similar circumstance, a woman named Ingrid protected my children and me from a dangerous situation.

In this chapter, I share stories of the women on the streets and explain the grace they bring to a troubled neighborhood. Meet Ingrid and Tanisha.

### *Silenced Voices – Protected by Ingrid – November 11, 2014*

I am proud that my two sons, Jaden (age 10) and Cole (age 7) share my desire to get to know people who society chooses to ignore. Together the three of us walked along Hastings Street, waiting for the right person to find us. As we passed Pigeon Park, a tiny woman of Aboriginal descent smiled at us from deep within her layers of clothing far too big for her tiny body. As we passed, she turned to others in Pigeon Park and shouted out, "Kids on the block," a custom I've grown to recognize, where the homeless and addicted shift their language and monitor one another to ensure their actions are appropriate for a younger crowd.

We continued to walk a few more steps. I asked Jaden if he thought she was the right person to join us. I knew he did, as he had the courage to walk over and talk to her while I waited a few steps back. He introduced himself and asked if she would like to go for lunch. As a sign of respect, she immediately put out her cigarette to stop the smoke from blowing near Jaden. I didn't hear the words but saw her smile and nod as he explained *Beyond HELLO*.

Together we walked and she introduced herself as Ingrid. She too had two children, ages 16 and 18—one boy and one girl. She reminisced about the days when she and her husband would remark that a life with two kids was like winning the lottery.

As we entered *Save-on-Meats*, most of the tables were full. The waiter offered us an L-shaped bench in the front bay window. We accepted and Jaden and Cole squeezed themselves down the bench to the far end. Ingrid sat between the boys and me.

Ingrid connected with the boys instantly. She laughed at their stories and decided that she too would love some fries. The boys ordered milkshakes and fries while Ingrid ordered an iced tea, fries and gravy. I asked how she stayed so thin with fries and gravy, as she peeled off layers to reveal a tiny figure framed by long, dark hair. She smiled and told me she was born weighing five pounds and has been tiny her whole life. She was born in Ontario and traveled to Vancouver decades ago. She gets to see her kids occasionally, but now that they are teens, they are busy too, so the visits are less frequent.

As we waited for our food, our conversation was interrupted. Ingrid was signaling to a man outside the window to go away. I hadn't noticed him. From outside on Hastings Street, he had spotted Ingrid eating with us. He stood pressed against the window, motioning for her to come with him. She waved him away again. She apologized and explained she knew him. I suggested he could join us if that was easier.

He entered the restaurant and threw money down on the table. He told me to buy my kids some ice cream. I offered him a seat and said he could join us. He decided to do so.

Ingrid shifted down the long table, and he sat at the end of the bench, closest to me.

He did not model the same grace as Ingrid. His voice was loud, obnoxious, and inappropriate for the restaurant. He ordered a coffee and fries while commenting that he was probably richer than me. I told him I hoped he was. He began to tell me he also had two boys, though he had lost touch with them. His behavior seemed to subside, and the inappropriate comments, which seemed to be his way of protecting himself, became further apart.

Instinctively, and without words, Ingrid and I assumed new roles. With a disheartened look of disgust for his behavior, her motherly instincts took over. She played eye-spy through the window with my boys, laughed with them and pointed at a car across the street being towed away. I knew she was keeping them busy, so they would not hear his words. At times, Ingrid would glance back and try to get my attention. She would add a comment and try and resume our conversation, yet each time he would put her down, call her an Indian or speak louder to silence her voice. Her eyes lost hope, and yet she continued to laugh with the boys and protect them from his words.

I noticed he wore a poppy, something you don't often see amongst the homeless community. Hoping for a positive twist, I asked about the poppy on his jacket. His eyes filled with tears and rage. He grabbed my arm with an uncomfortable grip and asked if I understood. He informed me that he was an ex-Navy Seal. He fought in Vietnam.

I did not understand, nor do many in my generation. I understand the idea of war, but luckily, I have no experience that could compare to his pain. I cautiously replied, "I don't understand, but I do appreciate your service. It's a world I can only imagine."

My words seemed empty to him, and he continued to talk, distracted by his own memories of destruction and thousands of lives lost. He had to kill. It was his job. With anger, he told me he fought so my kids do not have to. For some reason, he meant this literally, and he seemed angry as he looked at my boys. They did not hear his words. Ingrid continued to protect them by keeping them busy. I knew she could hear him, and I knew her intuition was to take care of my children.

He began to tell me about his two boys, now in their fifties, living in different cities. He softened and explained the beauty of the river, meandering through Quebec City. For once, my instinct told me not to offer to find his family as I often do on the Downtown Eastside. In his next breath, he asked me if I could try and find them. The request caught me off guard as he had no way of knowing that I often try to do this. His voice softened, and I searched Facebook, finding pictures of one of his sons. Moved to tears and anger, he took my phone. I wondered if I would get it back as his grip suggested I would not. I offered to send a message, which we did through Facebook.

He left for a smoke, perhaps overcome with emotion, seeing his child for the first time in decades, perhaps overcome that someone was nice to him despite his gruffness.

I paid the bill and thanked Ingrid. She smiled and thanked me, knowing we shared the same feeling, disappointed that our conversation had been disrupted. I took a picture of her with the boys. As we stood to leave, he returned. He wanted his picture taken too, so his boys could see him. His intention seemed okay, so I sat with him to have a photo taken. In a minute that seemed to last way too long, things turned. In his aggressive nature, he used his words and actions to control the situation. We were not safe. He reached up and grabbed Cole by the hood of his sweatshirt, pulling my seven-year-old son towards him. As he pulled Cole's hood back, the zipper from the sweatshirt dug into his neck and cut the skin. I yelled as loud as I could, telling him to stop his behavior. The restaurant froze as I'm sure even the kitchen staff heard. I had to yell a second time to end the situation. We left as fast as we could.

I made a mistake and turned left, only realizing a block later that my car was to the right. We turned back, seeing that he was not on the sidewalk. Ingrid ran towards us. Although their friendship had a history much greater than ours, I knew right then; our bond was stronger. She told me to cross the street as he was still in the area. She apologized and asked if we were okay. She spread her tiny arms as a shield to the street telling us to cross so we wouldn't see him. As we left, she shouted, "I love you." I know she meant it. In that second, I felt the victimization that women must feel living in the Downtown Eastside, and I felt a mix of relief and guilt, knowing we could escape while others could not. I also felt the warmth of the neighborhood that I so often feel, as Ingrid did what she could to care for us.

As I glanced across the street and through the restaurant window, I could see him, his face buried in his hands. He didn't expect my reaction. Maybe it's been a long time since someone confronted him. Maybe it's been a long time since someone treated him with kindness. Maybe he did not have the skills to connect with children. I don't know. A victim of war, he has lost everything: his family, his business, and his ability to love.

When I see a poppy, I not only remember those whose lives have been lost in war, but also those who struggle upon return. Driving home, my sons and I found comfort with one another, and for a short time, I questioned if I would ever go back to the streets. I thought of Ingrid and the victimized women and decided I could not allow him to silence my voice. I knew I would go back.

### *Dignity Deserved – Dinner with Tanisha – March 17, 2019*

The sidewalks of Hastings were buzzing: addicts, dealers, misplaced tourists, hipsters and agency workers scurried up and down the street. Some took cover to avoid the unforgiving raindrops. Some appeared not to notice the spring rain and peddled a few more packs of cigarettes before seeking shelter.

Makenna, a grade 12 student, and I offered *Save-on-Meats* meal tokens to those who looked like they could benefit from a handout as we waited for the right person to approach us so we could go *Beyond HELLO*. I assured Makenna that we would know when we met the right person. We wouldn't feel nervous.

Tanisha sat alone on a bench at the corner of Main and Columbia. Strong yet weak, her defined arm muscles supported her tiny body in a black wheelchair. Together, Makenna and I walked up to her and asked if she would like a meal token.

*"Hell ya,"* she replied with a smile that let us know she was the one.

"Would you like to join us for dinner?"

"Even better! Of course I would. This is awesome. Would you be willing to push me?"

With rods replacing a femur, her leg no longer supported her, and a recently broken ankle amplified the struggle. She sat with her left side extended, making movement up and down Hastings quite difficult. As I pushed Tanisha's wheelchair, I leaned forward so I could hear her over the sounds of screeching cars, trolley-buses and drug transactions. Makenna followed behind us and returned smiles to those watching. One man asked if Makenna was old enough to be on the DTES—perhaps protecting her, perhaps showing too much interest in her. Makenna smiled back with confidence, identifying me as her teacher and assuring those around us that she was only in the neighborhood to help.

The staff at *Save-on-Meats* welcomed us as always, and we made our way to a table at the back. We didn't have to ask Tanisha for her life story; she offered it freely, happy to have made friends and thrilled to have some peace and security even if only for an hour.

"Can I have a milkshake if it's not too much to ask?"

"Yes, please order anything you like."

"Can I have a meal and waffles? I could take the waffles as dessert and eat them for my next meal."

"Yes, that's a great idea. Why don't you ask for your waffles to go after your dinner?"

Tanisha was overcome with gratitude. She smiled sincerely, her shoulders softened, and she eased into a temporary escape knowing all we wanted was friendship and conversation.

Tanisha has not always lived on the DTES. Born in Prince George, she is the oldest of thirteen children. Her mother, a street worker, escaped the sex trade of the city and moved to Vancouver Island. They are connected in spirit but lack the means to connect in person. Tanisha's dad died from suicide. Her babysitter from childhood went missing from the Highway of Tears as one of BC's many missing women cases.

By age fourteen, Tanisha was pregnant. Unable to keep her first baby, she longed for better days. By seventeen, she was working as a prostitute in Maple Ridge, BC but the small community did not reap profit the way Vancouver's streets could. At first, she found the nightlife exciting. Vancouver doesn't sleep, and Tanisha did not feel addicted to her lifestyle or drugs. Petite, blonde and athletic, Tanisha believed she had the beauty and strength to escape the lifestyle when she was ready.

At eighteen, Tanisha was ready for more. She fell in love and began a family. She gave birth to two boys, now ages five and six. Unfortunately, their father wasn't able to sway from trouble and went to jail for possession of a firearm. Tanisha managed to stay clean and support her children for the first three years. Life as a single mom caught up to Tanisha, and her addiction pulled her back to the streets. Her children, now in the care of the government, may not know how much they are loved. Her arms bear their names—one tattooed on each forearm. She smiled with pride, confirming she could not love anyone as much as her two boys.

I asked Tanisha where she hoped to be in five years. She talked about getting clean and getting custody of her children. She worries her degenerative health may prevent this. Although she describes herself as an addict, she isn't as far gone as many from the streets. She budgets her funds and balances her addiction with scarcity of consumption. She spends an average of $100 per year on clothing and $375 a month for rent at one of Vancouver's worst shelters. Her room is near the back door, where anyone can gain access. The lock is easy to manipulate, and her room is broken into continuously. She is equally scared of strangers as she is her boyfriend. Her boyfriend, diagnosed with multiple personalities, is her protector and her abuser. She never knows what to expect, but doesn't feel she can escape. His protection is worth more than the dignity it costs her.

Tanisha ordered a spicy chicken burger with poutine. As she began to relax, she removed her outer layers. Her turquoise tank and a beautiful smile lit up her face. Her arm muscles were sculpted from manually propelling her wheelchair. The addiction has paid its price, and it's hard to comprehend that she is still only 26 years old. Her name, given to her by her grandmother, means 'giver of life.' Despite circumstance, Tanisha's eyes still sparkle as she appreciates the little things. She exudes gratitude, speaks of her spiritual connection, and is acutely aware of energy in the room.

Tanisha removed one of her heeled boots to let her broken ankle rest. She explained her dilemma. She wants treatment, but hospitals don't weave well with addiction or loneliness. Her reliance on fentanyl keeps her on the streets. She feels as if she is not eligible for the same type of care as you or me. She is convinced the hospital's goal is to discharge her as fast as possible to make room for those more accepted by society.

I apologized for the judgment she faced and asked her if it bothers her that passing cars lock their doors in fear of her sheer existence. She shook her head no and said,

*No—that's not it. It's the access to service that hurts. Taxis won't stop for me. And if they do, they rummage through my purse without permission to make sure I have money. Hospitals don't let me wait with others in emergency. As soon as I arrive, I am put in isolation. It's not just the people who stare out the window—it's those that should be willing to help that don't.*

I asked Tanisha if she would like to connect again. She agreed eagerly, and we exchanged contact information. With a new lightness, and a brown bag full of Belgium waffles, she asked if perhaps I could drive her home so she could escape her boyfriend for one night. We spoke about meeting again soon as we said goodbye. She paused awkwardly and took a risk, "Can I ask you one more thing? If I decide to get the medical care I need, would you come visit me in the hospital? I hate knowing no one will visit."

"Yes, of course. I would love to visit and bring you anything you may need. It's the dignity you deserve."

> *"Each time a woman stands up for herself,*
> *without knowing it possibly, without claiming it,*
> *she stands up for all women."*
> *Maya Angelou*

# Chapter 7
## Pain

*"Don't ask why the addiction. Ask why the pain?"*
*Dr. Gabor Maté*

### Christmas Money

My mom made parenting look effortless. My childhood was rich in activities including piano, T-ball, swimming lessons, girl guides, and dance. My mom never missed a school concert or recital, and somehow found time for regular trips to our family cabin and special vacations to Disneyland. We were loved, respected and cherished.

My dad continued to drift in and out of our lives during our childhood. I remember visiting his apartment once. It was full of newspapers from the previous year, and everything seemed dirty and unorganized. When my dad made plans to take us somewhere, he would either arrive late or he would not show up. Christmas was the exception. Every Christmas, my dad would make plans to pick us up and drive us to his parents' apartment where we would spend the afternoon as a family. I didn't know my grandparents on my dad's side nearly as well as my mom's parents, but we still enjoyed going as they lived in a high-rise apartment building where the top floor had amazing views of the city and a shuffleboard table. I loved trying to beat my brother in shuffleboard. At the end of our Christmas visits, my grandparents would give Jeff and me each a Christmas card with $50 cash. As a child, this was an amazing gift! My imagination would race with ideas of what to buy.

# CHAPTER 7 | PAIN

On the way home from Vancouver, my dad would stop to get gas. He would fill his tank and then search the car for his wallet. Coincidentally, every Christmas, my dad would 'lose' his wallet, and we would have to lend him our $50 bills to pay for fuel. He promised to pay us back on our next visit. We trusted him, and we believed we would get our money back. Of course, we never did.

My pain does not compare to the pain of those on the streets. I am fortunate that disappointment and rejection was only a small part of my childhood as my mom made up for it ten-fold. Regardless, I was hurt enough to develop a strong sense of empathy and compassion for others in pain.

After meeting hundreds of people who are homeless, I am certain that no one loses their way by choice. Homelessness is not about a lack of housing. It's about rejection, pain and isolation. Every person I have met on the streets has endured significant trauma, almost always during their childhood years. I am well aware of my privilege and appreciate that if circumstances were different, I could be in their shoes. If we want to end homelessness, we will need much more than food and shelter. We need to heal the pain and restore a sense of belonging.

In the fall of 2018, I met Katie. Her story alludes to the pain that exists just below the surface.

### *A Little Gloss to Hide the Pain – Katie – October 27, 2018*

We are all a mix of our good days and bad, our regrets and our successes. Nevertheless, we hope the world sees our beauty. When I visit the Downtown Eastside, I usually give away food as a way to start conversation. This visit was different. A friend of mine donated bags of makeup samples. I was able to create twelve makeup bags full of beauty products. With makeup in hand, my intention was to focus on the women living on Vancouver's streets and invite one person to lunch to share her story. Grade 11 student Sophia joined me for the day. We walked the streets, gifting makeup bags, allowing women with irreversible trauma to hide their hurt and apply layers of beauty. Rich or poor, lipstick and mascara can create the illusion of a happier, prettier self. We can hide dark circles, illuminate our skin and show the world the person we want to be. Underneath the sparkle, every woman has a story worth hearing.

Vancouver's roughest street is predominately male, and many women do not walk alone. We approached women surrounded by men and offered them makeup bags. Women smiled, and so did the men, knowing it was a gift appreciated by their female friends. As one woman looked up from a cold sidewalk and smiled at us, there was a moment of sisterhood, a moment where we understood the makeup might provide some relief to her cruel reality. Or maybe it was the recognition that makeup provides all women with a mask to hide behind, allowing us to create the story we want the outside world to see.

As we walked down the sidewalk, a young woman walked towards us. Her skin suggested she had not spent too many years on the streets, yet her slightly disheveled look made it all too obvious that the Downtown Eastside had become her home. As we were about to pass, I asked if she would like some makeup, and began to reach in my purse to pull out a cosmetic bag. With slight confusion and a polite smile, she said, "I would like some, but I'm a little short on cash these days." I smiled. "Don't worry—it's free." Later at lunch, Katie reminisced about the moment we met and laughed, "I was confused. You two didn't look like you would be selling on the street."

Together, the three of us walked to *Save-on-Meats*. Katie let us know she had been on the Downtown Eastside for five years. At age 28, she had lost too many friends to fentanyl overdoses. Her concerns were valid. In 2017, BC set a disturbing record of over 1500 overdose deaths in one year. Her ex-boyfriend, known for his alleyway graffiti art, stays in touch with her and makes sure she is aware every time a friend dies. Unfortunately, this happens far too often. Midway down Hastings Street, hundreds of stuffed animals hang from branches of a maple tree. Each stuffy represents a life lost. Commuters smile at the tree full of childlike toys as they race downtown. Only those who know the streets understand what the tree represents to the Downtown Eastside community.

While most of us enjoy running into old friends, Katie explained that there is a relief that comes when she sees someone she hasn't seen in a while. If someone is missing, her community doesn't assume they are busy—they assume they are dead.

Katie shared the struggles she faced when a more recent ex-boyfriend became abusive. Attempting to chip away at her self-esteem, he continually put her down and assured her she would be nothing without him. She eventually laughed, realizing she had survived every day before she met him, so she could probably survive the days after him, too. Her sense of humor showed her hope and resilience.

Katie did not grow up in poverty. In fact, her story is far from it. Like growing numbers of youth today, her unhappiness comes from an upbringing rich in material goods but lacking in solid connections. Growing up in West Vancouver, the richest community in BC, she describes her childhood as a bubble, with friends driving luxury vehicles as their first cars. By high school, her parents had divorced, her mom had become what she describes as a 'lush' drinking a '26'er' per night, and Katie had connected with drug dealers and found her way into alternate school. She remembers the kindness of the cop who recognized her from a school presentation and was particularly thoughtful after picking her up for her only charge of shoplifting.

These days, Katie sees herself as a lucky one. She has a job helping others in the safe injection site. She feels a sense of community and has many friends who accept her.

Katie is hopeful that she will be able to see her son soon. At age 10, he is being raised on Vancouver Island by her father and stepmother. She beamed with pride as she shared a story of her son using his words to solve a dispute on the playground. Katie was slightly discouraged as she has temporarily lost touch but hopes her twin or two older siblings may be able to help get her reconnected. She dreams of a brighter future, with business ideas to help others.

As we shared stories, Katie sipped her root beer and rationed her chicken waffles, saving half for later. She called us 'refreshing' for promoting good in the neighborhood. We asked our waiter to take our picture, celebrating our new friendship. Katie paused for a second, "Oh wait. Let me put some makeup on first." A little gloss was all she needed to hide her pain and show beauty to the outside world.

*"Fear, to a great extent, is born of a story we tell*
*ourselves, and so I chose to tell myself a different story*
*from the one women are told. I decided I was safe,*
*I was strong, I was brave."*
*Cheryl Strayed*

# Chapter 8
## A Sacred Spirit

*"She only nodded. It's all we are in the end. Our stories."*
*Richard Wagamese*

### The Power of Storytelling

In Aboriginal culture, it is believed that storytelling is the most powerful way to teach children, pass on legends and strengthen relationships. On the Downtown Eastside of Vancouver, over thirty percent of people struggling with homelessness and addiction are Aboriginal. Some have grown up in foster care, while others have survived the horror of residential schools. Each person has a different story, yet they share a collective pain. We all feel pain the same way. While many are addicted to drugs, the drugs are merely a Band-Aid for deeper wounds. Drugs offer a temporary escape from reality.

If we truly want to help, we must change the way we respond. We need to start to address the emotional needs. As Aboriginal culture suggests, storytelling is a powerful way to teach, to heal and to learn. It empowers the storyteller to find their voice, and it captures the listener and leaves them a little different than they were before the story began. I know these stories from the streets have changed me. I hope they change you, too.

In this chapter, I will share the stories of two of my favorite women, Lilly and TJ. Both have strong connections to their Aboriginal heritage and have taught me to live with greater awareness and connection to our world. Here are their stories:

# CHAPTER 8 | A SACRED SPIRIT

### *Lilly's Flower Shop – November 9th, 2013*

Meet Lilly, a strong, beautiful Aboriginal woman who offers light and warmth to the Downtown Eastside.

Around noon, I picked up my former student Anoop and headed to the Downtown Eastside. Anoop asked how we would pick the one person to join us for lunch. I let Anoop know we would walk the streets and say hello to people and when we felt like it was the right person, we would ask them to join us for lunch. When we arrived, we walked up and down Hastings Street for five to ten minutes. We smiled at many who recognized us. It seemed the streets were full of people who had written cards with us at Christmas or Mother's Day with *Project HELLO*.

As we approached the 'mall' (which is the roughest block of Hastings), we passed a lady who I recognized from our previous visits. She smiled and offered, "Be careful down here. There's a full moon, and they are crazy today!" We smiled and explained a bit about our project. She beamed with motherly pride as we shared our work. She introduced herself as Lilly, and we invited her to join us for lunch.

As we approached, we saw that *Save-on-Meats* was boarded up, closed for renovations. However, next to it, a newer restaurant, *The Lost and Found Café*, was open. The name alone seemed like a natural fit for our project, so we entered the café. Lilly, Anoop and I ordered lunch and found a table near the window; a table where looking one direction showed the harsh realities of Hastings Street, yet looking the other way offered the cozy sanctuary of a modern café.

Our lunch arrived, and Lilly began to share her story. Lilly is a citizen of the To-quaht Band, one of the smallest First Nations, situated between Ucluelet and Port Alberni, BC. She grew up in Port Alberni on the reserve, with few restrictions. As she recalled, you could drink and party at any age. By grade six, she was drinking alcohol regularly, and she stopped attending school. Her mother would come in and out of her life but spent most of her time in Seattle. Her father worked in logging, so he was not able to be around much. Her grandparents stepped into a parental role raising Lilly and her siblings. Lilly and her grandmother had a special bond. Even though there were eight children in the house, her grandmother would always wake up Lilly in the middle of the night when she had a special story to share. She would put the kettle on, make some tea and wake Lilly saying, "I don't like sitting alone. Let me tell you a story."

Lilly relished these moments and would awake from deep periods of sleep to hear her grandmother's stories: stories her grandmother passed down from her own childhood. I smiled and told Lilly a little about my grandparents and the special memories I have spending time with them. I understood completely the bond she spoke of. Lilly also shared a story of a dream she had one night as a child, a dream that one day she would have her own flower shop. Lilly found comfort in the images of such a dream.

Lilly's grandfather on her father's side was Chief in Ucluelet, and therefore some of Lilly's childhood was marked with ceremonial traditions. When she entered womanhood at age twelve, her band celebrated that very day with a 'Coming of Age' party. Her brothers dressed in wolf regalia and were instructed to be next to her; two on her left and two on her right. They had to follow her for the day and sit together at the community hall. Lilly remembers this as a powerful experience, yet also a challenging day for a twelve-year-old to endure when she wanted to run and play.

Unfortunately, these days did not last. After her grandfather on her mother's side died, the government stepped in and found new homes for Lilly and her siblings. Some went to live with aunts, while Lilly and one of her sisters were put into foster care in Cumberland, BC. They were placed with a Caucasian family who treated them well and had strong religious values. After about four months of living with them, the family let the girls know they were going to take a drive to Port Alberni to return bottles at the bottle depot. They asked the girls if they would like to accompany them and visit their relatives in Port Alberni. The girls agreed and traveled to the reserve to visit. Once arriving, Lilly and her sister went to see their childhood friend, Leon. Leon's family hid the girls so they would not need to return to foster care.

This left Lilly experiencing a range of emotion. Why did the government need to find her a new home in the first place? Why was it so easy to escape? Why didn't she ever hear from her foster family again? As Lilly struggled to find answers, she found comfort in a relationship with her friend Leon. When she turned 16, her father asked her and Leon to come for dinner. During dinner, he let them know it was time for them to be married. Lilly was married to Leon for six years, yet by age 22, she needed to escape his cycle of drinking and abuse. She recalls one evening when Leon dragged her out of a community dance by pulling her hair. Leon's older brother stepped in and beat Leon, threatening to hurt him again if he ever hurt his wife. Ironically, Leon's brother had also beaten his wife; however, when he saw his younger brother repeat the cycle, it helped him stop his own violence. At 22, Lilly knew she needed to leave the reserve to feel safe. She had two children with Leon, but Lilly was raising them on her own. When Leon returned to town, she let him know it was his turn and she needed to take care of herself. She headed to East Vancouver, following the path of her thirteen-year-old sister.

When Lilly arrived in East Vancouver, she played a motherly role towards her younger sister, who was actively using drugs. Lilly was determined to stay clean and managed to do so for two years. One evening, Lilly and her new boyfriend went for drinks with another couple. The other couple offered them 'Ts and Rs' (Ts and Rs are also referred to as 'the poor man's heroin.' The T stands for Talwin, a painkiller, and the R for Ritalin, a stimulant. When injected together, they produce a high similar to the effects of cocaine mixed with heroin). To Lilly's surprise, her boyfriend said yes, letting her know for the first time that he had a history of drug use. Wanting to know what her sister experienced, Lilly decided to try her first hit. The experience made her incredibly sick, yet she recalls waking up the next day, feeling like her mind had taken over her body, and she craved more.

Lilly's sister prostituted to earn money to buy drugs and pay her rent. Eventually, her sister and the sister's boyfriend told Lilly she needed to start paying more if she was going to continue to live with them. Her sister convinced her to turn her first trick and work the street corner. Craving the high of Ts and Rs, Lilly decided to work the corner once to get the money she needed. Now, three decades later, Lilly's eyes watered as she told us about her first night working the street. She had never felt so much shame. Despite the money she earned, she remembers bypassing the drugs and racing home to the bath to wash her body and drown herself in tears. Her need to feel clean surpassed her need for the drugs that night, yet a cycle had begun—a cycle hard to escape.

Like many girls working the streets, Lilly eventually learned how to separate her emotions from her experiences. She found a job working for an elderly couple, shopping, cleaning and running errands. At night, she would work the streets. One day the man she was cleaning for stopped her and said good morning. When she replied pleasantly, he said, "Oh, it's nice to see you. I can distinctly tell the difference between the three of you. I can see in your eyes who you are today." Like many sexual abuse victims whose stories I have heard, Lilly began to take on different personalities as an escape from the pain.

At one point, Lilly freed herself from the DTES and returned home to see her grandmother. Lilly was addicted to drugs and down to 80 pounds. When she returned home, she slept for days, withdrawing from the Ts and Rs. Her grandmother wanted to know why she was sleeping so much, and then all of a sudden eating so much. She told her grandmother everything. Her grandmother didn't judge. Instead, it brought them even closer. Lilly would sit for hours at the big window in her grandma's front room watching an eagle. Lilly knew that the eagle was a symbol of honesty and truth.

When the eagle appeared, it granted the freedom and courage to look ahead, as the eagle represented the messages of the spirit. The eagle, the highest-flying bird, had the closest connection to the creator. One day, her grandmother sat beside her and offered wisdom.

"Lilly, I want you to make me a promise."

"What, Grandma?"

"No, Lilly. I need you to promise first."

"What?"

"Promise me first, and then I can tell you."

"Okay, Grandma. I promise."

"When I am gone, I don't want you ever to come back here."

"Okay, Grandma. I promise."

And so, when her grandma passed, Lilly left, and once again returned to the DTES of Vancouver. Torn between two lives, a Nation with family history yet plagued by alcoholism or her sister in Vancouver and the cycle of addiction.

For 29 years, Lilly has survived the streets of the Downtown Eastside. She has survived prostitution, heroin, cocaine and Ts and Rs. Somehow, she has overcome most of her battles. Five years ago, she successfully completed re-hab. She chooses to stay in the neighborhood she knows, perhaps because it is home, perhaps because she is drawn to stay. In Lilly's words, "This street grabs hold of you; the demon is the rock (cocaine)." Yet, Lilly has beat most of her battles and now feels compelled to help others.

At age 55, Lilly has gone back to school. She attends three days a week learning basic computer skills, and she plans to study Aboriginal law, eventually. Each day she walks Hastings Street while reciting positive affirmations in her mind. She stops to give hugs to so many who need it. Last year, as she walked the street of her neighborhood, a man from a church group stopped her to talk. He could tell she was a part of the neighborhood but that she was clean. He asked her why she stayed. Lilly told him she didn't know. He then said, "I can see why you are here. You have something important to do here. People will listen to you. You have a story to tell." As she told us this story, Lilly beamed with pride as she has believed this to be true. I told her about my blog and asked if I could share her story. With excitement, she replied, "You don't have to ask me twice!" She asked me what my astrological sign was and smiled as if she already knew when she discovered we were both Leos. As we finished our lunch, she sat in contentment and offered this: "We met for a reason. There is no such thing as a coincidence." I told her I couldn't agree more.

I asked Lilly two final questions. First, I asked what she would like others to understand about the DTES.

"It's not what people think. The people down here are real. They might be messed up, but what they say is real and true. Before you judge, try to walk a day in their shoes."

I then asked Lilly where she plans to be in five years. Despite her promise to her grandma, Lilly feels compelled to help her band. First, she will stay in Vancouver to finish course work and improve her employment skills and understanding of Aboriginal law. In time, she will make her way back to

Port Alberni. Her Nation, To-quaht, recently reached a treaty settlement with the government, and they are beginning to develop their oceanfront land and create employment opportunities. Lilly will use the funds she receives from the treaty for retirement and to set up a RESP for her grandson. Lilly smiled with adult confidence. Her eyes sparkled, and she reflected, "...or maybe I'll follow through with my dream as a child and open up my flower shop."

I can't help but wonder if Lilly's flower shop already exists in a metaphorical way. In Canada's darkest neighborhood, she is light. Her hugs, her stories, and her courage make a positive difference and offer beauty and serenity just like a fresh cut bouquet of flowers.

### Four Days – Meeting TJ – November 22, 2015

In late November of 2015, I was downtown with students, searching for someone to take to lunch, but I could not focus. I hadn't seen Noelle (the first woman we connected through *Project HELLO*) in almost a year, and I was worried about her. I needed to know if she was okay. I asked my students if we could stop in at her shelter. I knew Noelle preferred the outdoors to the stale air of the shelter. If she wasn't outside, I worried she must not be well. The students I was with had not met Noelle, but they agreed to come with me to check in on her.

We entered her SRO Housing on Hastings Street, and I asked the lady working the front desk if she knew if Noelle was in her room. She looked at me, not knowing what to say, and asked if I would wait for TJ. I agreed, not knowing who TJ was.

A few minutes later, the elevator door opened and a woman in her 30's walked towards me. When TJ saw me, she started to cry and shake. *"How did you know to come? It's you! You are the one from the Angels of Mercy story. We prayed for this!"* When we had reconnected Noelle with her daughter Natalie, *The Province* newspaper ran a front-page story entitled, *'Angels of Mercy.'* Noelle had kept the article on the wall of her tiny room.

Two days prior, Noelle had passed away from heart complications. Not knowing who to call, TJ (Noelle's support worker) had read the article from years prior. She held a smudging ceremony acknowledging Noelle's death and prayed I would come to the shelter. In Aboriginal culture, at the time of death, Mother Nature takes the physical body, and the spirit stays for four days before the Creator takes the spirit to its original form. To honor Noelle's spirit, TJ had left Noelle's room untouched. She asked if I would go to the room with her. Once we entered the room, TJ held another smudging ceremony, burning cedar and using an eagle feather to cleanse the room and connect us with the Creator. She explained Noelle's spirit was still there and she would know we were together. We were Noelle's two closest friends.

Days later, Dini, one of the students who had first helped Noelle reconnect with her daughter, returned to the shelter with me. We met TJ, and together we packed up Noelle's tiny, 6 ft. x 6 ft. room. We boxed up items to send to her daughter Natalie and bagged other items for disposal. TJ offered me Noelle's dreamcatcher, one of my favorite possessions that hangs on my office wall next to angel wings, made for me by a friend when we first found Noelle's daughter Natalie.

As we packed, TJ told us her story. Years prior, she had worked the streets as a prostitute. Noelle assumed the role of mother to all the working girls. They lovingly called her "Little Mamma." They would come to her for comfort and advice. One evening, TJ's pimp broke her jaw, and TJ ended up in the hospital. It was the same night her best friend was abducted from the streets and later, found dead. TJ knew she had to change her life and escape prostitution, or she too would be killed. TJ turned to Noelle for encouragement. Noelle helped TJ escape the streets and enter rehab. Years later, TJ secured a job as a support worker in the shelter, where life came full circle, and she was able to care for Noelle in her final months.

TJ planned a beautiful ceremony to say goodbye to Noelle. Little Mamma was loved. A community of students, educators, nurses, support workers and people living on the streets joined together to share stories, experience a final smudging ceremony and release Noelle's spirit back to the Creator.

*"So come, my friends, be not afraid. We are so lightly here.*
*It is in love that we are made. In love, we disappear."*
*Leonard Cohen*

# Chapter 9
## Fame & Fortune

*"When you realize nothing is lacking, the whole world belongs to you." Lao Tzu*

### *Lessons from the Lottery*

Years ago, I attended a lecture at the University of Victoria. While I don't recall the topic of the lecture, I recall a story the professor shared with us. He spoke of his previous job as a professor in Manitoba. Winters were extremely cold, and days felt long. He found himself at the lotto center on a regular basis, hoping he could win the lottery to fulfill his dreams. One day, he stopped himself in his tracks and asked some hard questions:

What would he do if he won the lottery?

What steps would he need to take to create the life he wished for?

Why wasn't he doing those things now?

He dreamt of the day he could move to the West Coast of Canada and be close to the ocean. He let his unlucky lottery tickets hold him back. When he stopped to pause, he realized he was leaving his life to chance rather than taking steps to make his dreams come true. He began to apply for jobs on the West Coast, and within a few years, his family started to live the life they dreamed of.

Since hearing this story, I always pause before buying a lottery ticket. When I crave the escape a winning lotto ticket could bring, I ask myself a few questions. What am I chasing? Why do I feel the need for more? What steps are in my control? Sometimes it's easier to dream than it is to stop and evaluate. Unfortunately, winning the lottery does not guarantee happiness. Fame, nor fortune, is enough to guarantee a sense of belonging. Human connections and love will always matter more.

The people along Hastings Street are often thought of as unskilled or uneducated. Stereotypical norms of homelessness prevent society from seeing clearly. Many of the men and women I have met on the streets have great accomplishments. Some have been married, some have had successful careers, some have university degrees, and some have served in the line of duty. Ron and Trevor demonstrate that fame, nor fortune, is enough to escape the loneliness of the streets.

### *The Boxer's Paradox – Ron Wilson – February 9, 2014*

There is something about boxing that captures the essence of being human. Boxing is brutal and graceful, painful and magnificent, terrible and triumphant. The same can be said about life in Vancouver's Downtown Eastside. Sitting on a cold bench in Pigeon Park, Ron Wilson knows he is in one of the most beautiful cities in the world. He knows what it's like to live the high life, experience glory, and feel the sun against his face. He also knows what it's like to get knocked out, hit rock bottom, and sleep on a cold park bench in sub-zero weather. And yet, despite the punches life has thrown him, Ron Wilson is my kind of champion.

You see, Ron Wilson is the first professional athlete my two young boys have met face to face. They got to shake Ron's hand, learn how to box, watch YouTube clips of archived boxing fights, and hear the stories from a legend. My boys made a new friend and smiled ear to ear because they decided to join my husband and me on a family outing, going *Beyond HELLO.*

As we walked towards Pigeon Park, I wondered if the right person would appear. As I turned away, my nine-year-old son Jaden spotted a kind-looking man who he felt was the one. He asked me to step closer and say hello. I did, and to our delight, Ron said he was hungry and eagerly accepted our invitation.

As we made our way to *Save-on-Meats,* we all introduced ourselves, and Ron commented on the cold, and what it was like to sleep outside at night. Cole, my youngest son (age 7), quickly tried to relate and told Ron that sometimes he likes to camp in the backyard. Ron smiled, and together, we suggested that camping would be better in warmer weather. My husband Shawn asked Ron where he was from and almost immediately, Ron began to share his life story: he was born in Vancouver, but left to live in California for 30 years, before returning to his home city.

As we entered *Save-on-Meats*, the boys excitedly picked out a table with stools. Shawn, Cole, and Jaden sat on one side of a pub-style table, and Ron and I sat on the other. Together we ordered burgers, fries, onion rings, and milkshakes as we slowly defrosted from the outside temperatures.

As we waited for lunch, Ron continually thanked us for taking him out. His voice was humble, soft-spoken, and rich. His eyes twinkled in the warm air, and you could see that a weight lifted as he engaged in youthful conversation with my boys. Ron agreed with Jaden that he should avoid my request for a much-needed haircut, and he shrugged his shoulders and tilted his head in a smile when we talked about how much the boys hated vegetables.

As we ate our lunch, Ron spoke of his life story. He grew up in Burnaby, BC attending McPherson Junior High and Burnaby South Secondary. We quickly realized he was at Burnaby South at the same time as my mom, Shawn's dad and their siblings. Shortly after high school, Ron became a professional boxer. He began his career in 1967 with the South Burnaby Boxing Club. After competing in the BC Golden Gloves tournament, he headed south to California. He competed as a professional boxer, earning up to $5,000 per fight. He got to see the world and compete in auditoriums throughout the USA and Australia. Together with his wife, he had two children, a boy and girl. He was living the American dream as a pro-athlete and he was having success. He fought in over 500 rounds, winning over 70 percent of his fights. In a controversial match in 1972, he lost a fight to Chris Finnegan. Though 42 years later, Ron suggests it was a controversial ruling. He still believes he won the fight. Ron took a moment to watch the fight via YouTube on my phone but passed the phone back after a minute, perhaps because he had the visual already or perhaps because it was a painful memory.

Unlike most conversations of *Beyond HELLO*, I decided not to ask too many questions. It was apparent that life had knocked Ron down a couple of times for him to find his way to Vancouver's Downtown Eastside. I asked if he had contact with his children. He said his son was 44 and his daughter was 39, but explained he didn't know if they would want to hear from him. I told him I was 39 as well. He paused for a second, smiled, and said, "Then you can be my daughter." I smiled back and said, "Well, that's perfect because I don't know my dad, so you can be my dad." He liked that.

As we finished our lunch, the boys asked if they could take a picture with their new friend. Ron's eyes lit up again, and he quickly put his hands in position, ready for his boxer's photograph. The boys giggled and learned how to put their fists up too. As I took a couple of snapshots, the three of them pretended to box.

When it was time to go, Ron thanked us again and shook all of our hands. He looked me in the eye and said, "You are a blessing." Then as he slipped out the restaurant doors, the boys turned to the glass window and tapped it, wanting to have one final look at their celebrity. Ron playfully tapped back and walked away with a youthful bounce in his step. At least for today, Ron was once again a professional boxer.

A few moments later, after paying the bill, we walked as a family, heading back to our car. Ron was with some friends, back on his bench in Pigeon Park. Although it had only been minutes, Ron laughed and said, "Hey, great to see you guys!" He introduced us to friends, thanked us one more time, and stood up to give me a hug. As we agreed to meet again, he said three words: "I love you." Maybe it was for his 39-year-old daughter. Maybe it was for me. Either way, in that moment, it was right.

Driving home, we reflected as a family. Shawn loved the experience, making note that he loved it a hundred times more than he had expected. Never had he entertained the thought of meeting a pro-athlete on Hastings Street. Jaden loved how friendly Ron was, and how much he could tell that Ron had liked him. "Mom, it's nice to know that it's not always the way it seems." Cole, at age 7, added, "Mom, I want to see him again because I can tell he has a heart, and we got to hear interesting stories." We drove home, happy to have a new friend, and confident we would return to that park bench to meet up with our favorite boxer.

### *Searching for Happiness: Life in Reverse – Trevor – July 19, 2014*

What if you were born with everything you had ever dreamt of? What if you had your health, an abundance of money, a home overlooking the ocean on Vancouver's Westside, and opportunity at your fingertips? Would you be happy? Would you have found what you are searching for? It's a life most of us only dream of. It's the reason we buy lottery tickets or tour the prize homes. It's a world we imagine where we would not have to worry about the rat race of life, a place where we believe we could find happiness. But what if you were given all of this as a child? Would it mean as much?

Meet Trevor. Like many whom I meet on the streets, Trevor defies conventional stereotypes. He has not been forgotten, he did not grow up in poverty, and he does not shoot up with needles. He chooses to seek solace in what most describe as Vancouver's darkest neighborhood. Perhaps it's here that Trevor can rebel against society proving that money cannot buy his happiness. Perhaps it's here that Trevor can search for self-acceptance and carve out a life where he feels a sense of worth. Perhaps he escapes the judgment, the expectations and pressure to be someone others want him to be.

Trevor does not want self-pity. He knows he has lived a life with opportunity afforded to few. He has traveled the world, attended a prestigious university, married, had a child, owned property and had an abundance of wealth at his fingertips. Despite living the dream, he openly admits his ex-wife was right—his first love is the bottle.

Today Trevor lives an eclectic life, merging his riches from the past with his chosen poverties. He knows he does not have the ability to manage his own funds, and so instead he rents a room in Vancouver's Eastside. On his modest income, he spends his days eating healthy (juicing his own foods), reading for hours a day, and escaping from the world with his drug of choice: alcohol.

Unlike many of the DTES, Trevor doesn't speak with resentment or hatred towards his family. He fondly remembers his ex-wife's beauty and intelligence, and he beams with admiration for his daughter's success and achievements. On a scale of 1-10, she is his 17. He makes it clear to us; it is of no fault to anyone but himself that his daughter does not talk to him anymore. His alcohol addiction caused too much harm. And while Trevor keeps the conversation light and comical, you can see the tears surface quickly as he allows himself to feel the guilt that comes with destroying a family.

As we walked together down Hastings Street, cars raced by, heading to the downtown core in search of success. To the passerby, Trevor is nothing but a drunk. But maybe Trevor has lived his life in reverse. Starting with everything, he now chooses to have nothing, and in his absence of stuff, he speaks passionately about what really matters. For Trevor, everything is nothing, and nothing is everything.

Trevor is finding his way to happiness. Well-read and able to quote practices from positive psychology, Trevor stands on Hastings Street offering a blend of compliments and comedy to everyone who passes by. Local business owners and residents of the DTES neighborhood smile as they wander by, knowing well that Trevor will brighten their day with jokes and witty sayings. In Trevor's words, he is on an all cheese diet, one where he can make cheesy jokes for hours at a time, beginning most sentences with "Hey, let me tell you my favorite joke." In fact, this is how we met Trevor. Shortly after parking our car, my friend Jenny and I made our way towards *Save-on-Meats*. Trevor intercepted our walk to tell us that we were more gorgeous than Hillary Clinton and Jane Fonda. (I should add that when he switched from sunglasses to reading glasses at lunch, he shouted out, "Holy crap! You just got twice as big!")

As we walked to the restaurant, Trevor was proud to tell us his favorite jokes, yet aware enough to notice that a slightly overweight, shy-looking woman was walking towards us. He stopped his jokes with a polite, "Excuse me," and shouted out to the girl, "Hey, you are beautiful. Don't forget that!" She turned back with a slightly uncomfortable smile showing that she wished his words were true in her eyes. He quietly turned to us and said, "I hate it when girls have low self-worth!" For the next two hours, Trevor entertained us with a blend of life stories, great jokes and his mantra, "We are here for two reasons: we are here to achieve an abundance of love and an abundance of honesty—that's it! An abundance of love and an abundance of honesty."

As lunch came to an end, Trevor called over the waiter and asked if he would take a check. The waiter paused with thought. Trevor chuckled and told him his check would bounce so hard it would break the window. He then broke into a comedic jig, offering dance lessons to the adjacent table. Despite Trevor's scattered blend of comedy and life lessons, there was an irony to Trevor. Often making fun of himself, Trevor would like you to believe he is simple. And yet his knowledge of the world, impressive vocabulary, and understanding of everything from politics, literature, art, government and psychology make me believe Trevor has a gifted mind.

I asked Trevor his favorite place he has traveled. He laughed and said, "Main and Hastings" (the main intersection in the Downtown Eastside of Vancouver). Of course, he is joking, but I wonder if perhaps this has some underlying truth as this is the corner where Trevor has found acceptance.

I then asked what he does not like about the neighborhood. He looked at me with an answer suggesting the superficial nature of my question: "Other people search for happiness. I can see a thousand sunsets vividly when I close my eyes. I don't need to go anywhere. If I have a loving thought, I'm grateful. If I have an honest thought, I'm grateful. And hey, if I have an intelligent thought? I'm surprised!"

Lunch with Trevor was fun. He kept us laughing, he kept us entertained, and we became friends. In two hours, we went *Beyond HELLO* and heard a story worth hearing. Between Trevor's jokes, he took some risks, and together, we sent a message of love to his daughter in Ottawa. Trevor paused long enough to acknowledge we understood him when Jenny asked the hard question of why he did not accept himself. The hurt lingered, and it was clear that a life of privilege was nothing without loving relationships. When we said goodbye, Trevor joked about bringing us both back to his room. Underneath the joke, loneliness hung in the air giving us a glimpse into Trevor's search for connection. Trevor offered us more than we had expected: an abundance of love and an abundance of honesty. Maybe that's what we should all be searching for. When we can fall asleep at night, able to love ourselves, maybe we have found happiness. Maybe that is the true essence of success.

*"When I had nothing to lose, I had everything.*
*When I stopped being who I am, I found myself."*
*Paulo Coelho*

# Chapter 10
## The Invisible Fence

*"I always wonder why birds stay in the same place when they can fly anywhere on the earth. Then I ask myself the same question." Harun Yahya*

### *Limits We Set*

We are all creatures of habit. For the last twenty years, I have started each morning with a grande, half-sweet, nonfat, extra-hot chai tea latte from Starbucks. I certainly don't wake up craving chai, but I do crave my routine. I love saying hello to the barista, I love savoring the first sip, and I love feeling the warmth of the white cup in my hand as I drive to work or begin weekend errands. I am sure I would like other teas from other shops, but I am comfortable with my habit. Routines help ground us and create a sense of organization in our lives.

Understanding my habitual behavior helps me comprehend why Vancouver's homeless rarely venture from the Downtown Eastside. Within a six-block radius, over 2000 people sleep in shelters and alleyways. An invisible fence seems to surround them. The ocean is two blocks to the north, the city center is two blocks to the south, and Stanley Park is six blocks to the west. However, these areas represent belonging and freedom, something the people on the streets do not feel they deserve.

Leonard, Nathan and Cindy have helped me understand how lonely and isolating the streets can be.

### *Living in a Lonely World – Leonard – July 22, 2018*

On this particular day, a grade 12 student, Hudson, joined me to go *Beyond HELLO*. We started out by entering Cindy's SRO housing to pass on a message from her daughter. It was Hudson's first time inside a shelter. Like many, he expected to find humane living conditions, so the stale air, sticky floors and damaged walls came as a surprise.

After knocking on Cindy's door and not finding her at home, we left a note and carried on. As we were about to exit, a gentleman organizing his backpack in the stairwell shouted out "Be good, and always listen to what your parents tell you—they know best."

I laughed and said, "Most of the time—but not always."

I asked if he knew Cindy. He did, but he wasn't sure where she was on this particular day. He introduced himself as Leonard and quickly began to share his history: born in Sooke, BC, he had struggled with a difficult life. He worked hard fishing, made some poor choices, spent some time in jail and learned life lessons the hard way. Now at age 51, he wants to make his parents proud. He respects his parents and hopes one day they will see the good in him. He no longer jaywalks since being hit by a car, no longer steals since his grandmother gave him words to live by, and no longer wants to be judged because of his past. We let Leonard know we were headed to *Save-on-Meats* for milkshakes and asked if he would like to join us. He shook his head and said the *Ovaltine Cafe* is the place to go for milkshakes—even the glasses are better. We smiled and said, "Then let's go there!"

Leonard began to worry about his possessions. With no working lock on his door, leaving his possessions behind was not a safe idea. The shelter did not offer storage space, so getting ready to head out was an ordeal. On top of this, as we were about to go, he noticed a friend entering the shelter with a bike. His friend's room was on the eighth floor, and in 86-degree heat, getting a bike up eight flights of stairs would be a challenge. He asked if he could help out his friend before heading out with us. We agreed and offered to meet him on Hastings Street once he was ready.

For the next 15 minutes, we handed out bottles of water on the street. When I was about to look for someone else to chat with, Hudson encouraged me to stay, adding "I'd feel bad if we left, and he came out two minutes later!" Hudson was right. Two minutes later, out came Leonard with his life's possessions: a bike and a shopping cart of supplies. The shopping cart contained tools, bike parts, spare change, smokes, random clothing, and his favorite snack: apple juice and chocolate. With pride, he taught us how to wet the side of the juice carton so the chocolate bar label would act as an adhesive and bind them together.

I wondered how Leonard would travel on his bike with so much stuff. He attempted to walk his bike with one hand and direct the heavy cart with his other hand. Hudson offered to assist. Minutes later, we were walking up Hastings with Leonard guiding his bike and Hudson pushing the shopping cart. I asked Hudson if he thought anyone was looking at him strangely. He said no. That didn't surprise me in a neighborhood that is far less judgmental than most. I chuckled to myself, wondering how a one-day school field trip had become a decade long project where my student was helping push a homeless man's shopping cart up the road. This was surely a day Hudson would not forget.

As we crossed over Main Street, Leonard paused to point out the building to the north where words of inspiration were etched onto the cement balconies: Hope, Dignity, Work and Courage. Leonard let us know he pauses here every day and finds the strength to stay on the right side of the law. Years ago, when his arm was injured, his grandmother told him to get an empty cart and start collecting cans and bottles. She told him that if he pushed through the pain, he would not only strengthen his arm, he would earn money in a respectable way. He followed his grandmother's advice and prides himself on working for his money rather than stealing from others.

We reached the *Ovaltine Cafe* to find it was closed. We paused while Leonard greeted people by name, saying hi to most people who passed. Amidst the conversation, Leonard asked me to move my cell phone from the side pocket of my bag to an internal compartment. He didn't want anyone stealing from me. On what most perceive as BC's most dangerous street, we once again found respect and kindness.

I worried about Leonard trying to walk all of his possessions down to *Save-on-Meats*. He explained it would be easier to pedal his bike and push the cart at the same time, but he would need to go ahead of us. We made plans to meet him there. With grace, he peddled away, managing his bike and shopping cart.

As expected, *Save-on-Meats* welcomed us to their restaurant and allowed Leonard to bring his bike inside, while storing his shopping cart in clear sight of their front window seat. Leonard excused himself to wash his hands before our meal. When he returned, he continually thanked us for our time and company. He was thrilled to learn that Hudson was the runner up on *Chopped Canada,* a teen cooking challenge. As people would pass by, he would call out, *"Do you know who this is? He's from Chopped Canada!"* Leonard, who liked to cook, loved being in the company of a future chef.

We asked Leonard how he ended up in Vancouver. A self-declared "Sooke boy," he shared his journey from Sooke, BC to Edmonton, Alberta where he lived on the streets. He built his own temporary housing equipped with a portable heater and allowed working girls to stay in his hand-crafted shelter, providing them with a safe place to sleep. He spoke of his flirtatious nature and respect for women. He claimed he was too shy to 'make a move' or land himself a girlfriend. In Edmonton, he met his one long-term girlfriend. Together they moved to Vancouver. She entered rehab, and his bad choices got him three years behind bars. When he left prison, he reunited with his girlfriend on the DTES. He was disappointed to learn she had sold her rings for drugs and had fallen back into her addiction. Soon after, the unimaginable happened—his girlfriend, like many women from the Downtown Eastside, went missing, and was murdered.

I asked Leonard if he would ever leave the Downtown Eastside. He wasn't sure. For now, it was his home. Disconnected from his family, he spoke of the grief he felt learning he was not invited to his brother's funeral. From a family of seven, he described himself as the black sheep of the family. At age 51, he still hopes he can make his parents proud. Unfamiliar with Facebook, he did not realize the ease of finding family. Within minutes, I was able to show him pictures of two of his sisters. He teared up and asked me to send them messages, telling them how much he loved them. He also wanted to let them know that if any men were bothering them, he would still be willing to step in and kick some ass.

Misunderstood and distrusted, Leonard felt judged by the outside world. While he was open about big mistakes in his past, he was determined to let his grandmother's words of integrity guide him. He thanked me for lunch and let me know that he didn't shy away from hard work. He offered to help me out with yard work if I ever needed it. I thanked him and asked what he wished the world knew about him. He laughed and offered this:

*What I wish? Wishing is witchcraft. I don't believe in wishes. But I do believe in blessings, and my grandmother reminded me I am blessed, and I will see that in my 40's or 50's. I am 51 now, and I am not who I used to be. I don't fight, I don't steal, and I collect cans. I am blessed.*

He walked with us a while, asking if we really had to go. I promised to connect again in the future and thanked Leonard for his time and for sharing his story. We spoke of *Beyond HELLO,* and I let him know his story would help others understand. He asked me to check my phone one more time in case his sisters had replied. I assured him I would be in touch as soon as I heard from them. We said goodbye, as he balanced his bike and shopping cart, clinging to his possessions for comfort in a lonely world.

### *The Courage to Say HELLO – Nathan – August 18, 2015*

Why is it that sometimes the ones we love are the hardest to reach out to? Lost in our feelings of doubt or insecurities, many of us use silence as a way to protect ourselves. Worried about what others may think, we play it safe and avoid difficult conversations. Sometimes it takes courage to say hello.

On a hot summer day, in 2015, my friend Soni and I headed to the streets of Vancouver's Eastside to hand out water to the homeless during the mid-day heat. After some friendly conversation and banter with the livelier than normal crowd on the streets, we met up with my dear friend Ron Wilson in Pigeon Park. Ron, the professional boxer, had joined my family for lunch two years prior. I sat down beside Ron and let him know that my blog post about him had reached an old friend of his from California. I read him the message, and together we reminisced about his fascinating life story, a timeline inclusive of a professional boxing career, owning a tire shop and opening up a sports bar. On the other side of the park bench, Ron's friend Nathan sat listening.

I asked Ron if he had called his daughter since we had last spoken. He looked at me and said that he couldn't because he didn't have the phone number. I read an email to him from his daughter, encouraging him to reach out. He smiled, hearing about his three grandchildren. Once again, I wrote down his daughter's phone number. He planned to call. Just not right away. A wave of shame clouded over, and Ron decided to head home to his shelter for an afternoon nap. As we said goodbye, I asked Ron who he thought we should take for lunch. Ron said he wasn't sure as he scanned the crowded benches in Pigeon Park. Quietly, his friend Nathan spoke up and said, "I'm hungry." Soni and I asked Nathan if he would like to join us for lunch. Nathan accepted, and so together we said goodbye to Ron and headed to our favorite diner.

As we walked up the street, we learned that Nathan was originally from Edmonton, Alberta. Since 1997, he has been living in the SRO low-income housing on East Hastings Street. He has ventured back to Edmonton a few times to visit with his mom. Despite the harshness of the Downtown Eastside, Nathan is positive, gentle, and kind with his words. He loves Vancouver and is happy despite having so little. Nathan was appreciative as he ordered a strawberry milkshake and a double bacon cheeseburger with fries and gravy.

I asked Nathan if he had any children. Quickly he replied, "Yes, two boys, age five and nineteen." I asked if he got to see them much. As he looked down, he told us no—he had not met them. With a hint of optimism, he let us know that one day, he hoped to meet his sons. I asked Nathan if he would like me to help find them. Shame took over, and he mumbled a polite "No thank-you" and returned to his milkshake.

After a few more sips, Nathan offered more. He mentioned to us that his oldest son's mother had contacted him this past year and said their son wanted to meet his dad one day. I asked what his son's name was and used my phone to see if

I could find him on Facebook. In an instant, I found his son's profile. We asked Nathan if he would like to see a picture of his son. Right away, he said yes. We asked if he was sure, and his eyes began to sparkle with the anticipation of an expectant parent. I reached my phone across the table, and for a long moment, we sat in silence as Nathan saw his son for the first time.

When I put the phone down, and we began to talk again, Nathan asked if we could go back to the photo. With wonder and love, he repeated, "Can I see it again? Can I see it again?" Like a new dad wanting to hold his newborn in his arms, Nathan wanted to hold my phone. Beaming at the noticeable resemblance, Nathan held the phone with his son's profile picture up to his cheek, and we used Soni's phone to take their first photo together.

We asked if he would like to reach out and send his son a message. With confidence, he said yes, and together we drafted a beautiful note, letting his son know that Nathan hoped to travel to Edmonton to meet him.

As lunch ended, his son had yet to receive our Facebook message, and so we said goodbye and promised to be in touch. Smiling ear to ear, Nathan let us know he never thought today would be the day he would see his son for the first time.

An hour later, Nathan's son contacted me. Overwhelmed by the news, he let me know it was a lot to take in. I explained our *Beyond HELLO* project and told him that if and when he was ready, we could help him connect with his dad. Within minutes, he replied that he was ready, and together we decided that Soni and I would head back to the DTES to reach Nathan so they could have their first father-son phone call.

Two days later, after 19 years of silence, Nathan found the courage to call and say hello.

### Loved and Alone – Cindy – August 13, 2016

Imagine for a moment that you live in Vancouver's SRO housing. Rats and disease run rampant. Violence, addiction, trauma and poverty plague the streets. You can't remember the last time you slept soundly, and when you do find security through the attachment to others, you take on their burdens and worry for their safety as well as your own. This is the hell that Cindy awakens to every day. The building she lives in no longer meets the standards of even an SRO project, and a tear down in the future is inevitable. Imagine when you write your address down for someone, you actually write the words 'Blood Alley' as your street name.

Now imagine the bittersweet mix of emotions that come from learning you do have four siblings who love you but don't know you. Sisters that have learned of you from your birth father who spoke of you with love while raising his new family.

Imagine seeing photos of women who resemble you, except their hair is gorgeous, long and flows effortlessly. Imagine seeing your own eyes on a familiar but unfamiliar face— your eyes—in a different place and time, living under very different circumstance; sisters, who unlike you, avoided the family cycle of addiction.

It's hard for me to articulate what I experienced as I caught up with Cindy over breakfast. The morning started with pure joy. Cindy was awake by 6 AM and arrived early at *Save-on-Meats* to get us a seat. Excited to learn more about her family, she was filling in the waiter before we arrived. As we approached, Cindy was at the restaurant door doing a full arm wave. *Project HELLO* student, Miranda, had done some research and had found Cindy's sisters living in Ontario. I had called ahead to let Cindy know we were coming to share the news with her.

We let Cindy know that we had phoned one of her sisters on the way downtown. Her sister had agreed to stay by her phone so we could text or call when the time was right. Moved to tears, Cindy decided we should text so she could think about what to say. She recalled a moment the month before where she had a strong feeling she had letters to write, but she was unsure who she was supposed to write to. She kept a notepad and pen near her bed, waiting to write letters when the time felt right. It became clear that she was ready to write to her sisters.

We texted her family and asked for their mailing addresses. Hoping they would reply during breakfast, Cindy eagerly ordered a chocolate shake and a Belgium waffle with berries and whip cream. She explained she tries to be healthy, but this was a day worthy of a big breakfast.

Shortly after breakfast arrived, the texts began to roll in. Her family asked if Cindy would like to see pictures. Cindy accepted the offer. She smiled ear to ear, ready to see the faces of her siblings.

Tears streamed down her cheeks as she saw the resemblance, especially with one sister. Cindy asked about her father's resting spot. Learning that he passed away while on vacation in the Yukon, Cindy remembered her father's dream of seeing the Northern Lights. She smiled, knowing his dream came true. She held my phone and cried, looking at a photo of her brother. Her sister shared that he had died a year earlier, succumbing to his alcohol addiction.

The photos of nieces, nephews, aunts and uncles continued to arrive. Picture after picture showed families who looked well-put-together. Family born to the same father, but living completely different lives. Cindy, who struggles from concurrent disorder (mental illness and drug addiction), became overwhelmed. Although she continued to eat her waffle, she was only present physically. I waited. I had seen this before and understood that Cindy could easily slip in and out of coherence, and in and out of depression. As we finished breakfast, joy returned, and Cindy stated it was a good day to go for a drive. I let her know I had brought her a bag full of clothing and a new book, *The Maze Runner*. Perhaps we could go for a short drive before taking her home. We headed to the car.

As we drove through Stanley Park, I don't think Cindy saw the scenery. Perhaps it was a defence mechanism blocking the images of freedom as cyclists, runners and tourists navigated the seawall. Perhaps it was mental illness. Regardless, Cindy needed to talk, needed to find meaning, and needed to understand her life on a spiritual level. We listened as Cindy talked, though we also knew she was in her own space and speaking more to herself than to us. She spoke of

God and powerful moments that prove to her that a higher power exists. She spoke of her stubborn streak and suicidal ideation and the knowledge that a power greater than her has kept her here. She spoke of suffering and her belief that through suffering, we find appreciation, love, and compassion. She spoke of her dislike for most doctors (who have no basis for understanding trauma) except for Dr. Gabor Maté. She sees that he understands suffering, and has suffered himself, and is therefore respectable as a doctor. She skimmed the back of her new book, *The Maze Runner* and remarked, "That's like my life. Trapped. Stuck in a maze. That's me."

As we drove back to the Downtown Eastside, Cindy emerged from the place she had been and verbally acknowledged the shift. Laughing out loud, she shouted, "Wow. That was crazy! I'm back to reality now!" She looked at me and said, "We are both truth seekers. We feel things to understand." I smiled and told her I always find her quotable. She spoke of old souls, so I asked if she thought she was an old soul. She thought about it, smiled, and responded, "I am not sure, but I like to question the questions, so maybe I am."

Blood Alley was closed to traffic, so we pulled over on a side street, and Miranda and I hugged Cindy goodbye. She lifted the big black garbage bag full of clothes and flung it over her shoulder. She clenched her new book with her sister's contact information secured inside. Like a recording, she said out of habit, "Could you spare any change? I'm hungry and could use some food." Knowing her stomach was full, but that her next meal would not come as easily as mine, I gave her enough money for lunch and another big hug. In sweet sorrow, I drove away as Cindy's silhouette faded back into Blood Alley; loved and yet, alone.

> *"There is a crack in everything.*
> *That's how the light gets in."*
> *Leonard Cohen*

# Chapter 11
## Grit

*"Grit is living life like a marathon, not a sprint."*
*Dr. Angela Lee Duckworth*

### Tap'er Light

Growing up, I was lucky to have two amazing grandparents. My mom's parents, who we called Nanna and Pop, played a significant role in raising my brother and me. When my mom was busy, they would offer to care for us. Most Sundays, we would get together for family dinners. The summer months were my favorite as my nanna and pop would offer to take me with them to their family cabin. By age three, I would wave goodbye to my mom and head out of town with Nanna and Pop. Nanna was full of warmth, love and laughter. Pop resembled hard work, grit and resilience.

Summer days were filled with big breakfasts, long walks, boat rides and nightly card games. As we played outside, Pop would chop wood for the fire while Nanna would bake fresh pies. With six children and fifteen grandchildren, the cabin would bustle with the sounds of a happy family. Nothing was more important to Pop than his family, and his sparkling eyes let us see through to his soul. When it was time for us to drive away, Pop would wait at the door and holler out 'Tap'er light' as the car began to roll. It was his way of saying 'go easy on the gas pedal and drive safe.' If I close my eyes, I can still see his smile with his arm extended long in a wave, and I can still hear his strong yet caring voice wishing everyone love and safety.

Perhaps it comes as no surprise that something about Irvin reminded me of my Pop. With a similar build, a life of manual labor and a love for others, they both exuded grit. While Pop chopped wood to keep our family warm in the cabin, Irvin chopped wood for survival in the forest. Pop would yell out, 'Tap'er light,' just as Irvin would belt out 'Cowboy up!'

### *Cowboy Up! – Irvin's Rock – March 2010*

In late March 2010, after working in the local shelter for six months, I had a great conversation with Irvin about what he would do if he won the lottery. He spoke of all the charities he would give back to as he appreciated the help he had received from others. On our final evening at the shelter, I approached Irvin and told him I had a gift for him. I gave him a lottery ticket and told him I hoped his luck would change. I thanked him for sharing his story and for making such a difference with our students.

Irvin reached in his pocket and told me he had a gift for me as well. Not knowing what to expect from the pocket of a homeless man, I remember feeling nervous about what I was about to receive. When he unfolded his hand, he held out a small brown rock. He told me that the year before the shelter opened, he was living under a bridge in Port Coquitlam. Some middle school students had approached him with their teacher and offered him some cookies. With the cookies, they had also given him the rock and told him it was a friendship rock. They asked him to keep it in his pocket, and to remember each time he felt it, that the community cared about him. Irvin told me the lottery ticket would replace the rock, and he asked me to take the rock and put it in my pocket to thank me for caring about him. He asked me to remember that he cared about the community, too. Eight months later, Irvin passed away from his addictions and health complications. However, his story and his rock will be with me forever. *'Cowboy up!'*

I am grateful to Irvin for teaching me that every homeless person has a story worth hearing. We need to look beyond addiction to discover the root of the pain. Love, compassion and connection will always be more powerful than punishment, shame, or isolation. I am thankful to Irvin and my pop for modeling the perfect combination of strength, grit, love, and courage.

*"Only the gentle are ever really strong."*
*James Dean*

# Chapter 12
## Resilience

*"She stood in the storm, and when the wind did not blow her way, she adjusted her sails." Margaret Edwards*

### Together We Thrive

Why is it that adversity allows some people to thrive while prompting others to struggle? Before I began working with the homeless community, I would not have used the word resilient to describe people on the streets. By society's standards, they are people who have given up. Many believe homelessness and addiction are choices people make. Some berate the homeless and yell in frustration, "Get a job!" They refer to them as bums or hobos. Somehow, society turns a blind eye and pretends that homelessness is the fault of the people on the streets and not the responsibility of the community. We push the less fortunate away and forget about them, almost angry at them for being there. While most would agree it is unconscionable to discriminate by race or gender, discrimination against those on the streets remains. When we drive by, walk faster, lock our doors or refuse to make eye contact, we are part of the problem. For a culture to thrive, no one should be pushed out.

When I reflect on my life, I can think of moments where I have thrived and moments where I have failed. When I have been surrounded by support and encouragement, I have thrived. When I have felt judged and pushed away, I have failed. It's amazing to me that so many people on the streets find the courage to rise above the discrimination and continue on despite the judgment. Every time I take someone to lunch, I get a glimpse of their life, and as we say goodbye, I am well aware of my privilege as I get into my car and they walk back towards their shelter. I have the opportunity to escape. As long as we continue to exclude people on the fringe of society, few will break through the invisible fence.

Imagine my surprise when Cindy found the courage and resilience to break free, all on her own.

### *She Walks by the Ocean – Cindy – Summer 2016*

There's a certain serenity that comes from a walk by the ocean, a sense of comfort and peace that rejuvenates the soul. In late August, as a way of embracing the warm summer air and showcasing our beautiful city, I took our exchange student from Japan to Vancouver's seawall for a walk by the ocean and dinner on the beach. Together, we walked Price (our family's 100-pound Goldendoodle) along the shore. Accompanied by thousands of tourists and Vancouverites, we embraced the beauty of the day and watched the sun set slowly across the horizon.

Two miles away, another woman had the same idea. In search of serenity, she offered to take her neighbor's dog for a walk. Searching for a place of acceptance, she chose a lesser-known shoreline: the ocean's edge at the foot of Main Street, north of Hastings. Although she passed industrial lots and metal fencing, she experienced the same joy as she walked by the ocean. She heard the sounds of the waves, felt the slight breeze of a summer wind and watched night fall along Vancouver's shore.

Aware that our exchange student may want to buy some souvenirs, I offered to stop in Gastown. The streets were alive, and parking was scarce, but we eventually found a spot two blocks off the main strip on the periphery of the cobbled streets. Recognizing that the night was too warm to leave our dog in the car, I opened the hatch and invited Price to join us. The odds of passing another dog walker were slim in this retail strip. Urban sprawl has covered every available inch with concrete. Sidewalks, businesses, condos and industry left no space for grass. We began to walk along Powell towards Gastown. Meanwhile, the other woman strolled south on Main Street, making her way back home. As a relatively new dog owner, I was still learning dog-walking etiquette, but I recognized that most dog owners liked to greet one another, often letting the dogs sniff while the strangers exchanged pleasant hellos. As the other lady and I crossed paths, roughly ten feet apart, we smiled in acknowledgment as dog owners do. I kept walking in the dim light.

"Hello." Now fifteen feet away, the woman offered a friendly greeting.

I turned back, smiled again, and said hello back. I noticed that she looked happy and walked with confidence with her well-groomed dog (typical Vancouverite). I kept walking.

I heard her again, this time a little louder.

*"Hey there…"*

She stopped walking and turned back to call out. This time I recognized the voice: a friend from the past. Joy surrounded me, and my heart began to burst. There, on the corner of Gastown, was my friend Cindy. Cindy, the first woman brave enough to share her story with *Beyond HELLO*. Cindy, whose dream when we met in 2013 was to one day see the ocean. Cindy, who I drove to Stanley Park so she could dip her feet in the ocean, only to have anticipation turn to trauma as the laughter and delight of regular folks hit her like a ton of bricks. Cindy, whose addictions used to chain her to Hastings Street like an invisible fence. Cindy, a woman who has survived abuse, illness and addiction. Cindy, who my students helped reconnect with her daughter Paige. Cindy, who had endured years of homelessness. Cindy, who looked so happy and at peace that I did not recognize her. Cindy, who by a power greater than I can explain, kept stepping into my life at just the right moment.

My recent attempts to find Cindy had failed, and like many times before, I worried and wondered if she was still alive. This time, I didn't find Cindy. This time, she found me.

*"Individually we are one drop.*
*Together we are an ocean."*
*Ryunosuke Satoro*

# Chapter 13
## Men & Shame

*"Shame is the intensively painful feeling that we are unworthy of love." Brené Brown*

### Forgotten Phone Calls

I grew up knowing my father was a disappointment. By most accounts, he met the description of the typical 'dead beat dad': missed birthdays, forgotten phone calls, priorities other than my brother and me. At age nineteen, I let my dad know how I felt, how he had let me down, and why I was not going to be on the receiving end of a dysfunctional relationship. And that was it. No more phone calls or broken appointments—nothing. My brother has a much more forgiving soul and kept trying. Phone calls would come every year or two for my brother. Plans would be made, but more often than not, the plans would be broken. And yet, there were glimmers that my dad wanted to reach out. At different points in my life, I would learn that he knew more about me than I realized. He would mention achievements of mine to my brother or ask about my marriage or children (neither of which I had told him about). When I ran with the Olympic Torch for the opening celebration of the Vancouver 2010 Olympics, he told my brother he would call and ask if he could come to watch. The phone never rang. My phone did not ring for over twenty years.

On my 41st birthday, I was out for a family hike when my phone rang. Half way up to Quarry Rock, I answered my cell only to hear, "Happy birthday. It's your dad." Unexpected. Not prepared. If I had known in advance, I would have worried about what to say. I would have worried about how I would feel. I would have debated whether or not to answer the phone. Instead, I heard these words: *"I would like to see you one day ... I will call you again soon."*

After hanging up, I was happy he had called. I imagined the courage it took to pick up the phone. I wondered if the phone would ever ring again. Shame held him back and that next phone call never came.

I am not unfamiliar with the world of shame. Many of the homeless men I have met who live in the Downtown Eastside Streets of Vancouver are prisoners of their past. Even though many of them accept my invitation and mail heartfelt messages of love to their families at Mother's Day and Christmas, they will not open the door to receive love back from their families. It seems that time and time again when families contact me and ask their loved one to call, it's the men who say no. When I tell them I have found their families, their eyes sparkle and they want to know all about their loved ones. Some have even received offers to fly home to be with family. The men on the streets are cautious about reaching out, and most don't. They can't. I can only assume they blame themselves for the pain they have caused. They are burdened with guilt and shame and they don't want to cause any more harm. They usually feel they deserve the circumstances they are in. Instead of reaching out, they turn to their addictions or new friends to find comfort. In this chapter, I share some of the stories of men who struggle with addiction and the shame of letting others down. Leonard and Ron loved their families and wanted to reach out, but shame got in the way. I suspect the same was true for my dad.

## *Chivalry and Shame – Leonard – August 6, 2018*

Kaelen, an 11th grade student joined me for a trip downtown to let Leonard know we had been in contact with his sister. We first looked for Leonard on the streets, suspecting he may be easy to spot. Last month he had shown Hudson and me how he could balance his bike and shopping cart, a skill I cannot even imagine perfecting. We couldn't see Leonard, so we headed to his shelter around noon. He wasn't expecting us, so when we knocked on the door, he asked if he could have a few minutes to tidy up. He asked us to wait in the hallway. Through the door, we could hear intense scurrying and the sound of a handheld vacuum going on and off. Fifteen minutes later, the door opened, and Leonard invited us in as his guests. (When I say invited us in, I mean he opened the door with one square meter of floor space and gave us the tour from the doorway.) He was proud to show us his place: a residence the size of your average bathroom. I couldn't see a bed. I assume it was under the 5-foot pile of stuff. Country music played, cowboy hats were stacked on a high shelf, and multiple bags and suitcases leaned against one another holding his life's possessions.

As I introduced Kaelen, I mentioned that she is a cyclist. With pride, Leonard removed a few sheets draped over piles and eagerly bragged about his bike collection. Somehow, in his tiny space, he had a few bikes. He brought his 'Gary' bike to the hallway to search for the date stamp. He taught us about *Gary Fisher* bikes and gave us a quick history lesson on the evolution of mountain bikes.

Leonard had been awake for days. Sleep-deprived and hungry, he wanted a few more minutes to wash up before joining us for lunch. He needed sleep, but since he knew we had a message from his family, he was eager to head out and chat. He asked if he could meet us in fifteen minutes outside the shelter.

Leonard emerged in his best clothes. He wore new jeans, a fresh shirt and Australian hiking boots he had purchased on the street for $5. He offered to bike ahead and check if his favorite restaurant was open. He asked us to stay put so he wouldn't waste our time. We smiled and watched his bags while he biked up and down Hastings. After confirming that both the *Ovaltine Cafe* and *Save-On-Meats* were closed due to the holiday, Leonard asked if he could take us to his favorite chicken restaurant on Main Street. We politely agreed to try it out.

As we walked, we told Leonard we had messages from his sister. His eyes teared up and he could not wait to hear what she had to say. I told him his sister was willing to chat on the phone. He couldn't call. In an awkward dance of shame and chivalry, he offered, "No, not quite yet. How about I take you out for lunch? You took me out last time. This time it's on me!"

I'm embarrassed to say lunch was a struggle. The restaurant looked like the food inspectors had gone on strike or somehow missed this stop for a decade. In 86-degree heat, the restaurant offered little refuge and the food under the heat lamps looked like it had been there all week: chicken, fries, fish, Chinese food, macaroni, soup and lasagne. The owners were eating lunch as well. I took note that they had brought food from home in Tupperware rather than consuming their own cooking! Leonard ordered a plate of Chinese food and asked us to pick something. Sensing our trepidation, the owner let me know the fries were fresh. I said okay and asked for the fries, trying to be respectful. We tried not to insult Leonard and slowly ate some fries while he had his lunch. I assured him they were good.

During lunch, Leonard gave us the inside scoop about life on the streets. He spoke about those he could trust and those he couldn't. He blamed the alcoholics and heroin addicts for ruining the streets. An addict himself, he is off the needle. He feels a sense of success, knowing he no longer uses injection drugs. Despite his progress, he cannot tell me where he wants to be in five years as six months feels like a big goal for now. He explained how buying and selling of goods worked in the neighborhood. He asked if we had been to the 'mall.' I told him I was familiar with the block where people sell their goods (some stolen, some not). I asked who shopped there. He talked about the people who drive to Hastings Street to get goods at cheaper prices. I told him I wouldn't be comfortable buying stolen goods. He looked at me like I was crazy and said, "Who is going to know? Just me, myself and I." He tried to convince us that the bargains make it worthwhile and that we were crazy to spend more elsewhere. He asked if he could take us shopping, assuring us we would love the experience. He reminded us never to settle for the first price offered.

The 'mall' is the block I usually avoid. Selling is the focus, and there is a tension you can feel as people protect their goods, all eager to earn a buck. The street was incredibly crowded (like a shopping mall on Black Friday) with an eclectic mix of items: brand new camping equipment, clothes, shoes, new hats, computers, phones, flats of straw-berries and a strange collection of Costco deli items (meat, pasta, shrimp and seafood sauce) all nicely displayed on the hot sidewalk.

Leonard introduced us to vendors, all who politely said hello. He was proud to tell his buddies on the street that we were his friends, and he was our tour guide. He kept saying with surprise, "They have never shopped here before!" Despite Leonard's encouragement, I could not bring myself to purchase any of the products. One particular man looked like he was struggling more than others, so I offered him some change. Leonard, wanting to be our host, mirrored our actions and offered the same man some money. It was clear all afternoon that Leonard wanted to show us he could take care of us as his guests.

We took some photos, and I sent them to his sister. He asked me to point out to her that he hated his hat. A cowboy at heart, he kept telling us his hat lacked starch. His sister instantly replied and confirmed it was a dorky hat. He laughed, impressed with her banter. She sent her phone number should he wish to call.

I asked if he was ready. With a look that said it all, he smiled and said 'Nah.' Like most men on the streets, that step was better kept for another day. Chivalry and shame were enough for today.

### *Saying Goodbye to a Legend – Ron Wilson – October 3, 2016*

For three years, I visited Ron Wilson at his favorite park bench in Pigeon Park. Unlike some of the people I had met on the street, I always knew how to find Ron. Each day, he would sit with friends on the same park bench in Pigeon Park. Most days, he was dressed in jeans, a plaid shirt, and a baseball cap. A six-pack of beer rested at his feet. He would pace his drinks throughout the day and chat with friends or those passing through the neighborhood.

Each time I would visit Ron he would light up and ask about his daughter. Ron knew I had reached his daughter through social media, and he beamed with pride each time I told him she was doing well. When we would part ways, Ron would often tell me he loved me. It was like he displaced his love and treated me like I was his daughter. His family tried over and over, and I repeatedly wrote down their phone numbers for Ron. Eventually, he accepted a call from his son and daughter-in-law after I offered to dial and help with the introduction. Next, we planned to call his daughter. I knew this would be a big step for Ron. It was obvious he could not handle the hurt he had caused his children. He kept saying he would find the courage to call. Unfortunately, shame immobilized Ron, and he never picked up his phone.

Despite my hundreds of conversations on the streets, there is one thing I cannot get used to with *Beyond HELLO*. Too often, I am saying more than hello; I am also saying goodbye. Residents living in the Downtown Eastside are eight times more likely to die young than the general population.

In early October 2016, I was at work when I received a call from the Native Health office. A kind lady named Kim had read my blog about Ron and took the time to find me to let me know Ron Wilson had passed away.

While I have been moved by every story I have heard on the streets, there are four people who have really touched my heart. Irvin, Noelle, Ron, and Cindy have each made a significant impact on my life. I have had to say goodbye to three of them.

In 2012, Irvin passed away on the streets near the local community shelter. Three weeks prior, he was attacked by teens with baseball bats. While his death was ruled unrelated, I am sure his spirit was broken. His funeral was standing room only. Despite being homeless, Irvin had touched the hearts of many and connected a community.

In 2015, TJ had helped plan a beautiful service where my students and I said goodbye to Noelle, the first woman we reunited with family through *Project HELLO*.

In 2016, we said goodbye to a legend. To my own two sons, Ron was never a homeless man. He was a professional boxer and he was their friend. Ron holds a special place in my heart as I didn't choose Ron to go for lunch; my son Jaden did at age 9. For years my boys enjoyed visiting with Ron. They wrote about Ron for their school projects and tried to shift the perception of homelessness amongst children. I love the way Ron's eyes would sparkle when Jaden and Cole would visit. Despite Ron's setbacks in and out of the ring, he was a champion in our eyes.

### *It's All Good – Visiting my Dad – April 17, 2016*

When *Project HELLO* began, a few people asked me if my interest in this work came from knowing my dad was temporarily homeless. I have always answered no to this question and I still would. As an adult, I wasn't looking to repair my relationship with my father. In fact, saying no to that relationship was one of the best things I did to take care of myself. I was at peace with my decision.

I wasn't expecting the flurry of emotions that came when I received a call from my brother in April 2016. I picked up the phone to hear my brother say that if I wanted to say goodbye, I should head to the hospital as soon as possible as our dad was on life support in ICU and may not make it through the night. That's when the anger came. I didn't expect anger, but that is what I felt. This was it—the finish line, and he still hadn't found a way to reach out or apologize for never being there. I was furious.

Luckily the hospital was an hour away, so I had time to think about what to say. We were told that he could likely hear us but would not be able to speak. I drove and prepared for the one-way conversation. My drive to the hospital was when reality hit:

*I did not start Project HELLO because of my dad—BUT— my experience with Project HELLO and Beyond HELLO would help me heal my own soul and say goodbye to my dad.*

I thought of all of the men who wanted to reach out and couldn't. I thought of the messages of love they would write but could not say. I knew my dad was just like them. He never found peace in this world. I didn't want him to die that way, and so I decided I would ask him to forgive himself. He needed to know that neither my brother nor I carry the anger with us, and that we are and will be okay.

My brother and I met in the hospital lobby and headed to the ICU. Due to a shift change, we were asked to wait in a private ICU waiting area with one other family. As we walked through the door, I could not believe it. Standing in front of me was TJ, Noelle's caregiver from the Downtown Eastside. When Noelle had died, TJ had taught me the Aboriginal customs around death and had led me through my first smudging ceremony. Here, bracing another death, TJ once again appeared in my life.

As we sat in the waiting room, TJ and her mom shared the news that their nephew had been stabbed and airlifted to the hospital. As we waited, they taught us more about Aboriginal culture and made suggestions on how my brother and I should respond when seeing my dad. Their talk provided comfort, and I knew that once again, we were meant to meet.

When it was time to enter the room to say goodbye, a nurse escorted my brother and me to the private ICU room. We stepped inside. The skeleton of a body looking back of us had to be hours from death. Something seemed wrong. The hair was much darker than my dad's hair ever was. The facial structure didn't match. After my brother and I looked at each other in confusion, we stepped out and read the sign. The last name was three letters off my dad's last name. It was the wrong room.

We were re-directed to room #9. We were prepared to see someone in a similar state. What did we find? Another surprise. A nurse sat blocking the entrance and began to give us a medical update. I have no idea what she said as I was too busy staring at my dad, a man propped up talking on an iPhone. Hooked up to multiple machines, he was on life support, but he was having a conversation on a phone! A man in a green vest sat next to him. The nurse asked if I had any questions. I said, "Yes. Who is the guy beside him?"

"Oh. That's his nephew."

Huh? My brother and I are my dad's only living relatives. When he was a child, he lost one sister to cancer and lost his twin sister to suicide. He does not have any living brothers, sisters, parents, nieces or nephews. We said a polite hello and met a family friend who referred to my dad as his uncle. It turns out my dad and his fourth wife had sponsored a family to move to Canada from Bosnia. How is it that the same man who can't be a dad can sponsor others? Perplexing, but nice to see that he helped someone.

My dad looked up and made eye contact with me. We have the exact same green eyes. His eyes filled with tears, he reached for my hand, and he repeated over and over, "It feels like Christmas." (I glanced at my wallet, hoping he wasn't referring to the times he had robbed us of our Christmas money). He could not believe my brother and I were there. The love he felt for us was instant. He cried and cried and pulled us closer to him.

Amazed, I watched this person who I had always thought to be heartless have light, warm and even charming conversation with his 'nephew' and his nurse. It was comforting to see that despite his failed relationships with us, he had made some connections in this world. Minutes later, 'aunt and uncle' showed up. Confused again, my brother and I offered to step out for a while.

An hour later, my brother and I returned to find my dad alone. We each sat on one side of him. Initially, small talk prevailed, and he went on and on about the expensive parking we must be paying. He didn't like that he cost us money. His eyes would allude to more, and you could tell on multiple occasions that he wanted to say more but couldn't. I thanked him for phoning on my birthday and said it must have taken courage. He agreed it did while nodding and staring into the distance. He talked sports with Jeff and struggled to go deeper. He became incredibly uncomfortable and needed water, blankets, and help from the nurse. He winced in pain and struggled to breathe. And then it happened. With both of us at his side, he talked about how he knew he had grandchildren, and the knowledge that Jeff and I were happy was what he needed to be able to forgive himself. He apologized and told us he lived with guilt and shame every day for the type of father he was. We asked him to forgive himself. He kissed us both, told us he loved us, said how special we were, and let us know it was time for us to go. Jeff smiled and said to him, "It's all good, Dad."

As we walked away, he seemed comfortable. My brother turned to me and said, "Did you see how happy he was?" Later on, when we reflected on it, my brother said it was the first time in his life he could think of my dad and feel happy. From what we understood leaving the room, our dad could die any day. We left, not knowing if we would see him again. Although he was never able to be the dad he should have been, he had found some peace knowing we were okay. Jeff was right. "It's all good."

*"Give thanks for those who did you wrong. They unknowingly have made you strong."*
*Anonymous*

# SECTION

## CONNECT WITH COMPASSION

*"It's our collective strength that creates miracles."*
*Oprah*

# Chapter 14
## Human Connection

*"If there is any meaning in life, greater than connecting with other human beings, I haven't found it."*
*Melinda Gates*

### Genuine Conversation

It's hard to find time to connect. I am sure we all have friends that we have promised to make plans with, only to have days turn into weeks. Life gets busy, and sometimes finding time to meet friends, even for a quick lunch, can be difficult. We all go about our routines and somehow manage to overfill our days running from one commitment to the next. We have great intentions, yet finding time to sit and truly enjoy one another's company is a luxury we do not often grant ourselves. I am no different. No matter how many resolutions I set to live with purpose, act with intention, and be present, I still gravitate to somewhat meaningless time killers such as scrolling through social media or tuning into reality TV. I blur what matters with what doesn't. Although I can fill my time with meaningless activities or busywork, I recognize that there is nothing I enjoy more than deep, genuine conversation. Nothing matters more than human connection.

Perhaps that's why I am so drawn to the Downtown Eastside of Vancouver. On Hastings Street, the sense of urgency disappears. Technology is scarce, to-do lists do not exist, and there is no one to impress. There are no false pretenses, no fancy brand names, and no four dollar lattes. People are everywhere. People have time for genuine conversation, and they long to connect. Yet, in a cruel twist of reality, these are the people we ignore. We drive by. We lock our doors. We think of addiction as a choice, and we somehow justify that we are different than 'them.' We label them. Homeless. Addicts. Bums. Crack-heads. Hobos. After all, they are not 'us.' We could not end up there. Not only are we different from them, we know better. We credit our success to the choices we have made.

But what if none of that was true? What if each homeless person is our equal? What if each of 'them' demonstrates an admirable amount of resiliency simply for surviving the painful circumstances of their lives—circumstances we would not wish upon our worst enemy? What if each person wandering the streets deserved to be treated with empathy, love and dignity? What if every one of 'them' had a story worth hearing, a heart worth healing and a soul deserving of true human connection? What if they need more than food and shelter? What if they are just as human as you and I and warrant the respect and dignity that we grant our closest friends? What if they are worthy of our time to meet for lunch? To solve the pain of the streets, we need to connect with compassion.

In this chapter, I share stories of connection. Whenever I get overwhelmed or begin to think I have a stressful life, I head to the streets. The men and women who have lost everything have great perspective and know exactly what matters most. Mikey, Sheila and Garrett remind us that nothing matters more than human connection.

*In Search of Our Common – Circling with Mikey – November 28, 2015*

Remember when you were a child, and you would sing campfire songs that increased in length with each verse? Or how about the first time you tried to remember the words to the *Twelve Days of Christmas*?

Imagine if your mind worked that way, where each new thought surrounded the last and rather than moving from thought to thought, each conversation became an expanding circle, spinning, growing and anxiously holding on to where it began. That is how Mikey's mind works. Mikey is capable of listening, comprehending and communicating, but he processes in a complex way where everything repeats and circles around initial thoughts. Struggling with concurrent disorder, Mikey has his challenges. As a resident of the DTES, he is living in SRO housing where he does his best to fit in with others. In late November of 2015, he joined my husband Shawn and me for a walk-through Vancouver's crisp, leaf-covered streets. Rather than sharing my experience with you, I will share our story verbatim so you too can walk with Mikey. Here's my best recollection of our chat together:

"Do you have any spare change? Any spare change?"

"No, sorry. I don't have change, but I would love to buy you some lunch or a coffee."

"Oh, you don't have change; you don't have change … coffee. Hmmm." He looked down at his empty coffee cup. "You don't have change and I don't have coffee but how about a bus ticket?"

"Yes, we would be happy to buy you a bus ticket."

"Okay, a one-zone bus ticket. Can I get two? We can walk to 7-11. You don't mind? You don't have change, but instead of coffee, you will buy me a bus ticket?"

"Sounds great. Yes, let's walk to 7-11."

"Where are you from?"

"We are from Maple Ridge."

"You are from Maple Ridge, but you are in Vancouver, and I live here, but I am going to 7-11. I am from Steveston. But I lived in Coquitlam because I was at Riverview Hospital. But it is gone now, but I was born in Steveston. You don't mind buying me a bus ticket?"

"Sounds good, Mikey. Let's walk to 7-11 and get you a bus ticket."

"Do you have a job?"

"Yes, I work at a school."

"You have a job? I have a job. You work at a school. My job is to go to 7-11 and get a bus ticket. One-zone. I will go to see my dad. You have a job, and I have a job, and we are going to get a one-zone ticket, but I don't need a coffee and you don't have change. I went to UBC (University of British Columbia)."

"Nice! I went to UBC too."

"You went to UBC and I went to UBC, but I didn't go to school there. I went there on a bus. You went to UBC and went to school there, but we both went to UBC."

"Yes, Mikey. We both went to UBC."

Arriving at 7-11 together, he asked, "Can I get two? Two one-zone tickets? I don't need a coffee or change but can you buy me two one-zone tickets?"

We offered Mikey some food and some lottery tickets as well. The cashier rang up two one-zone bus passes, two lottery tickets and a slice of banana bread.

Mikey seemed flustered. "Two. Two. Two."

"Yes, Mikey. Two. Two one-zone tickets and two lottery tickets. Two. Two, all for you."

"Two. Two. Two."

"Yes Mikey—two."

We handed Mikey his new items and headed back into the crisp air.

"It's almost Christmas, and you bought me a present. This is a good Christmas. I am from Richmond, and you are from Maple Ridge, and we both went to 7-11. We both went to UBC. I have a job, and you have a job. Thank you, thank you."

"Mikey, have you ever taken a selfie?"

"A what?"

"It's when we take a picture together. Do you want to be in a selfie to remember our day?"

"Yes!"

"We are friends, and we walked to 7-11 together, and we both went to UBC, and you bought me bus tickets because you don't have change and I don't need coffee. This is a good Christmas."

With a fist pump and a smile, Mikey beamed as we parted ways. Hours later, when we looked at our bill, we realized why Mikey had been so flustered. "Two—Two—Two." Mikey was trying to be a good friend and save us money, only asking for what he needed. We accidentally bought Mikey two packs of bus tickets, not two one-zone tickets. Mikey had 20 one-zone tickets to circle around Vancouver. It was enough for him to gather many more stories. I smiled, knowing we would have much to talk about on our next visit.

### *A Sunday with Purpose – Meeting Sheila – December 2, 2013*

If you drive down East Hastings Street on an ordinary day, you can look out your car window and see the faces of people who have lost their purpose—lost souls who have traded away hope for a life on the streets. This particular December day seemed different. East Hastings was alive, and purpose was abundant. The streets were flooded with activity. Church groups handed out meals. The local bottle depot managed the crowds awaiting payment. Movie extras roamed the streets as a backdrop for a new film, and the Downtown Eastside Sunday Market was in full swing. It seemed everyone had a purpose or at least something to occupy their time.

I too had a purpose. My plan was to make not one but two new friends. You see, usually, I travel to the Downtown

Eastside with family, friends or students and invite residents of the Downtown Eastside community to go *Beyond HELLO*. I then share the stories through my blog. After reading my blog, a lady named Donna contacted me. She asked if she could go *Beyond HELLO*. She offered to pay for lunch in exchange for the opportunity to have a conversation with each other and hopefully with someone living in the Downtown Eastside. I agreed.

As Donna and I drove, we talked about family, health, spirituality, intuition, and our life experiences. Our discussion went well beyond the surface level conversations that usually occur when you first meet someone. Instead, we spoke about connections that exist between all people and the opportunities we have to act in significant ways. We agreed it was important to listen to your inner voice. By the time we reached the Downtown Eastside, we had a connection based on mutual respect and understanding.

We wandered through the street market, marveling at the collection of stolen goods being sold in an open marketplace. We considered offering lunch to some of the men who passed by with their life's belongings in shopping carts, but we didn't, as we both knew they would refuse. Leaving their carts unattended would be too risky in this neighborhood. We wandered back up Hastings and offered lunch to a few others who looked like they could use a meal. Everyone refused. It felt as though we were not meant to go *Beyond HELLO*. Before giving up, we decided to stand at a busy corner on Hastings and let others approach us. It was our last attempt and a less invasive approach.

Within minutes, a lady entered the crosswalk. As she got closer to where we were standing, she appeared guarded. With tangled hair and layers of clothing, she gave us a second glance. Her eyes softened, and I could tell she was just as curious about us as we were about her.

I said hello and asked if she was hungry. With a soft trusting voice, she let her guard down. "Yes. That's actually why I left my shelter. I'm cold, I'm hungry, and I was hoping I could find a warm meal." Together the three of us walked towards *Save-on-Meats*.

By the time we reached the diner, we were walking and talking like three long-lost friends. Sheila introduced herself and made sure she learned our names quickly. As we entered the restaurant, she commented on how nice it was and mentioned it might be an ideal spot to bring her boyfriend for his birthday on New Year's Eve.

The waitress explained they were renovating and had a temporary menu in place. We were invited to take mini clipboards and tick off the items of our choice. We could create our own breakfast, salad, sandwich or burger. Sheila suggested we take the forms to the table to sit down together and discuss our meal choices rather than completing the forms at the counter. Not wanting to ask if she was literate, I read the menu choices out loud, and together we decided what to order.

Sheila thought about a sandwich and referenced her need to be healthy, briefly reflecting on a time years ago when she worked as an aerobics instructor in Toronto. She thought a sandwich would be nice, but when I started to ask her about the different bread options and sandwich toppings, I could see the decision became too overwhelming. Between her cocaine addiction, methadone use, and slow recovery after being struck by a van, she struggled to stay with one thought for more than a minute at a time. Through our conversation, you could see her eyes fade in and out of awareness. In some moments, it looked as if she needed to sleep. In others, she was alive, present and willing to share with us.

Perhaps because of the perplexity of the order form, or perhaps because the smell of burgers and fries surrounded us, Sheila changed her mind from the sandwich form and said she would rather have a burger and fries. Donna agreed and ordered the same. Sheila asked if I would have a burger too. I explained that I needed to order a salad as I was halfway through a 12-day cleanse. As the words left my mouth, I recognized how shallow they seemed. Here I was, explaining to a lady who searched the streets for food why I was only eating certain foods to detoxify my body. And yet it also felt human to share. She smiled, and I laughed and said, "It's crazy, the things women will do!" She agreed and let me know she would put the ketchup and mustard on her burger herself. She then winked and said it was one of her secrets for staying thin.

The waitress arrived with coffee. Sheila's cup had an inch of space at the top for cream or sugar. Sheila let the sugar pour. She poured so much sugar that the coffee started to overflow. She mumbled about the cup being too full and stirred her new concoction: 3/4 coffee, 1/4 sugar. As she tried to steady her shaking hand, the coffee spilled. Donna and I wiped it up as she drank and poured some out into a water glass.

Sheila grew up with a military police father, where she was never sure if she should get closer or further away. She didn't connect with her mom and ran away from home a couple of times, but was always welcomed back by her dad. Her mom and dad grew apart, but this only brought Sheila and her father closer together. When her dad died from cancer, she was devastated and turned to crack cocaine to find comfort. As a server in bars, she made her way across the country, eventually finding her way to the Downtown Eastside. She fell in love but lost her partner to cancer as well. Despite her drug addiction, she continually referenced her mantra to 'stay positive and do not look back.' I asked Sheila how she managed to maintain an upbeat attitude in such a difficult neighborhood, to which she replied, "It's about God and staying true to my faith." She credited God with her strength, but also gave herself credit for her survival. She asked us to do the same. "You need to remember you are not where you are at just because of him. Promise me you will give yourself credit too." We smiled.

Sheila ate her burger and fries with urgency. Between bites, she would pause for a split second and ask what else we would like to know about her. She had questions about her current relationship and wanted our advice. Her boyfriend wanted to move in with her and had even discussed marriage, but something was holding her back. When I asked if he was the one, she laughed. Donna asked if he was the one for now, and she smiled, saying he was a good man who loved her. She talked about her own behaviors, commenting that many men would leave her, but he stayed. She then took the time to ask us if we were married and how we met our spouses. Fading in and out, Sheila seemed to enter and exit our conversation. On her next high, she raised her coffee cup in the air and offered a toast: "To happiness and meeting new people." Together we clinked our glasses, smiled, and enjoyed each other's company.

I ended with my usual question, asking Sheila what she wanted others to know about the Downtown Eastside neighborhood. She answered with this:

*"What we are missing is a place to talk. A place to clear your head and talk through problems. A place to feel safe and have real conversations."*

We smiled, knowing exactly what she was trying to say. At least this week, Sheila lived a Sunday with purpose.

### *We are All Lost Souls – Garrett – November 9, 2013*

In early November of 2013, I met up with Armin, a university student, who had started *Project HELLO* with me during his high school days. As always, we had no idea whom we would take for lunch. In a somewhat awkward style, we walked the first block observing the neighborhood. We tried to be unobtrusive, yet by the way we dressed, we stood out as strangers. With a pang of guilt, knowing we could not help everyone, we scanned hundreds of faces wondering whom to approach. A tiny, old lady in a yellow sweatshirt and messy ponytail caught our attention. Despite many missing teeth, her smile was radiant, and her eyes were alive. We approached and said hello. We introduced ourselves and asked if she would like to join us for lunch. She smiled her big, wide smile and explained she could not join us because she had already eaten and because she was busy working. We asked what she was doing. She told us she was selling drugs so she could get enough money to bake cupcakes. On the streets, she is known as 'Fudge.' She loves to bake, and if she sells enough drugs in a day, she uses her extra money to bake cupcakes which she then hands out on the streets. She beamed with pride as she explained how much people loved her cupcakes.

Fudge couldn't join us for lunch, but she was eager to spread our goodwill. She pointed to a friend of hers who was hunched over a walker. She introduced us to a quiet, humble man named Garrett. I have to admit, I may have looked past Garrett as he didn't stand out in the crowd. She explained our offer, and Garrett told us he would need a second to take it all in. He was stunned. He turned to us and said, "I don't know if I am the best person. I might not like the lunch they are serving today." We told him that he could order from the menu and he could pick his own lunch. With bewilderment, he told us he could not believe his luck as no one had taken him to a restaurant in fifteen years. In seconds, Garrett started to connect with us, weaving together his life story with historical facts about Vancouver. His only concern was that our lunch date might not be enough time for him to tell his story.

We entered *Save-on-Meats* and asked for a table for three. We waited a couple of minutes for a table to clear. Some restaurant patrons glanced inquisitively at Garrett's appearance. It was clear the drugs and street life had toughened his exterior. We made our way to a booth and glanced at the menu. With childlike enthusiasm, Garrett asked if it would be okay to order french fries and a milkshake. We agreed and placed our orders.

I explained *Beyond HELLO* and asked Garrett for permission to tell his story. Not only did he agree, but he was also proud of this new role. He let us know it was the first time he felt a sense of purpose since he worked at *Canada Post* as a mail sorter. Despite the circumstances and battles he faced, he always felt a great sense of purpose when he had a job to do. His face brightened as he told us eagerly about the places he worked: an extra on *Beachcombers* and *21 JumpStreet*, a security guard at *Expo 86* and a 20-year graveyard employee with *Canada Post*. "I'm a simple guy. I'm a passive person—just don't piss me off. All I ask from others is that they don't lie and don't steal."

Garrett grew up in poverty, living in one of Vancouver's first Co-op housing units with a single mother and three siblings. His father worked on the tugboats but was not around much. Garrett wondered if his father was still alive. His mother worked hard to raise their family, but she was not the warm and affectionate type. Garrett reflected on his childhood and how much his mom's hugs would mean to him as they were few and far in between. As he got older, his mom would say to him, "Let me put on the kettle and make us some tea." To Garrett, his mom's tea and shortbread cookies felt the same as a hug. This was something he missed dearly since his mom passed away. At the time of his mother's death, a falling out occurred between Garrett and his siblings. Battles over the will and the distribution of his mom's possessions left the family on bad terms. He has not had any contact with his family since.

Shortly after his mom's death, Garrett was in a major car accident. He was hit head-on. The impact caused his toolbox to fly from the seat and hit him in the head. It took emergency personnel hours to rescue him from the vehicle. Garrett endured a sixteen-hour surgery to overcome the impact. Miraculously, he survived. He walks with a walker and has a metal chest plate to help with stability. In addition to this, Garrett contracted Hepatitis C through a blood transfusion. As he told us this, he chuckled at the irony. He is now an addict on the Downtown Eastside, yet his Hepatitis came from a blood transfusion rather than a dirty needle on the street.

After Garrett's mom's death and his car accident, he struggled to find meaning in life. He questioned why he was meant to survive. That feeling lasted until the day he was at a local shopping mall and he met his soul mate, Sylvia. Like his mother's hugs, Sylvia provided comfort to his life. The two married and lived together in the Eastside of Vancouver supporting one another. In 2001, Sylvia became quite sick and required kidney dialysis. Garrett supported her around the clock helping with her medical care. One evening he asked a friend to help so he could go out for a couple of hours. He returned to discover his wife dead. His friend had decided it was best to end Sylvia's suffering. In an absolute rage, Garrett walked the streets for 72 hours, not knowing how to move forward. He turned to drugs for comfort. As described by Dr. Maté, heroin often provides the same feeling as a warm, soft hug—the exact feeling that Garrett was missing from his life.

As we reminisced, Garrett stopped to thank us. It had been a long time since someone had listened to his story. He openly admitted he was struggling with his mental health. With clear articulation, he disclosed, "I am my own worst enemy. I have seen the worst of myself. I haven't looked in the mirror for a long, long time, but I am ready."

We thanked Garrett for taking the time to tell us his story. I apologized openly to Garrett for the judgment and lack of understanding given to his neighborhood. He understood and agreed that more acceptance was needed. He then smiled and said, "You know we judge you too, right?" I ask him what he meant. He let me know that as I was approaching, his friends had wondered what I was doing. They could tell I was an outsider to the neighborhood. He told me that from my clothing and the way I held my notebook, they had determined I was either a social worker or a cop. I corrected him and let him know I was a high school vice-principal. His face lit up and he chuckled, "See! Exactly! A cross between a social worker and a cop!" I smiled at his wisdom.

Before leaving, I asked Garrett if there was anything positive about the Downtown Eastside. With his shoulders relaxed and a peaceful expression, he offered this, "Every day you can open your eyes it is a beautiful day."

We thanked Garrett for sharing his story. He thanked us, still amazed that someone had taken the time to buy him a meal and listen to him for a couple of hours. We left with a handshake and a smile, grateful that we had taken the time to go *Beyond HELLO*, genuinely connecting with a new friend over lunch.

*"Try to be a rainbow in someone's cloud."*
*Maya Angelou*

## Chapter 15
## We All Want To Be Understood

*"We readily feel for the suffering child, but cannot see the child in the adult who, his soul fragmented and isolated, hustles for survival a few blocks away from where we shop or work." Dr. Gabor Maté*

While the stories differ, the pain remains the same. Every person I have met on the Downtown Eastside is stuck in a place of trauma. Some speak of family dysfunction, others speak of physical, sexual or mental abuse. If we continue to treat homelessness or addiction with food and shelter, we will not move forward. Mental health services need to be as accessible as physical care. We need to recognize the need for belonging and begin to help people repair their emotional wounds if we want to see them reconnect with society. Driving by and locking our doors is not the response of a caring community. In Vancouver, we are in crisis. The winter of 2016 made this clear.

### *Nine Lives – December 17, 2016*

When we think of the expression 'nine lives,' we think of survival, luck and overcoming odds. Unfortunately, this particular week in Vancouver, 'nine lives' took on a new meaning. On Thursday, December 15, 2016, British Columbia broke a record for the most drug-related deaths in one day. Thirteen lives were lost due to overdose; nine lives from one small community, Vancouver's Downtown Eastside.

Unfortunately, the individuals who died that day are better known as statistics than human beings. Who were these nine people? What were their stories? What are their names? Were they loved? Did they love? Where are their families?

Although I am only connected to the people on the streets through five-minute conversations, card writing and lunch dates, it is enough to make me pause and wonder. Did I lose a friend that day? Did my students help them reach out to family? Do we have an unsent card yet to reach their loved ones? I stop and wonder, feeling the loss of a misunderstood community. I can only imagine what family members of the homeless must feel each time they hear stories such as this on the news. Was their loved one impacted? Did they survive? Will they even know?

I was disappointed when I read the national media coverage of this story. The stories focused on an epidemic, a health crisis, and a drug problem. With fentanyl linked to 60% of overdoses, there was a need for change. The health minister listed solutions: housing, healthcare, detox, recovery.

Solutions only work when we accurately define the problem. Despite what the media tells us, we do not have a drug problem. We do not have a health crisis. We have a people problem. We have failed to connect, and we have accepted a system that pushes the fringe of society out.

We have created an invisible fence between them and us, and we allow our most forgotten citizens to live in the V6A postal code vicinity, the poorest neighborhood in Canada. We have turned our backs, locked our doors, and blamed drugs for the destruction of human lives. Drugs provide a temporary escape from lives much too hard for most of us to even imagine. In the hundreds of conversations I have had on the streets, I have yet to meet an addict with a happy childhood and an easy life. Their stories of trauma have ripped them away from family, shattered their sense of worth, and introduced them to a world where drugs meet their unmet emotional needs.

We have created a human experiment where somehow, we justify a fishbowl neighborhood where our most marginalized citizens are set up for failure, and we watch from the outside, blaming them for their inability to thrive. When they die, we blame the drugs. As one addict so pointedly shared:

*"I'm not addicted to alcohol or drugs—I'm addicted to escaping reality!"*

Every drug user began their life in the same way you or I did. At one time, they had a mom and a dad. They entered this world with innocence and an innate desire to connect. Something has gone terribly wrong. We, as a society, have failed to meet the emotional needs of our most vulnerable citizens, and yet we blame them for their circumstances. To find a solution, we need to start asking the right question. As Dr. Maté often states, it's time to stop asking why the addiction, and start asking why the pain.

It's time to recognize that we need to help these individuals find hope, develop a sense of worth, and heal their souls so they can flourish. In one night, nine lives were lost. It's time we stop seeing statistics and start seeing people.

### *A Dose of the DTES – My Why – Spring 2019*

While many hope to escape from the Downtown Eastside, there is also a magic that comes from Vancouver's forgotten neighborhood. The streets are full of sincere people, raw emotion and soulful conversation. Problems are real, relationships matter, and everyone is accepted as they are. It's one of my favorite places to fuel my soul. It provides a clear perspective.

For ten years, I have found comfort in Vancouver's roughest neighborhood. Whenever I begin to feel sorry for myself or feel stress from my busy life as a wife, mom and school principal, I head to the streets. It grounds me and reminds me of what matters most. I leave knowing my 'problems' are of minor significance.

When I head downtown these days, I often join Cindy for tea, to catch up and connect. She always asks about my kids and loves seeing vacation photos. In March of 2019, Cindy and I met up at *Save-on-Meats*. It's where we shared our first lunch in 2013 and where we always go to catch up on life. She ordered her favorite vanilla milkshake with eggs, toast and a waffle. She was hungry and excited to enjoy a big meal.

Cindy has been trying to get out more, but life is expensive. A recent trip to a movie theatre and a day at Playland Amusement Park left her watching her last few dollars until her next welfare check arrived. Cindy dreams of the day she can move in with her boyfriend, but it's difficult to find housing for a couple, especially with their history of mental health and addiction. Both are clean now and cautiously optimistic about their future. Cindy let me know that although she is fifty, her doctor told her she has the heart of an eight-year-old. I smiled and told her it's from loving so much. And I meant it.

There isn't a nicer person in the DTES. Cindy greets people by name, offers hugs, listens intently and feels immensely. She has a beautiful soul. She has endured more pain than anyone I know, and yet she sees beauty. I reminded Cindy that meeting her has been one of the best experiences of my life. As we sat across the booth from one another, Fleetwood Mac's *Don't Stop* began to play. Cindy began to sing:

*If you wake up and don't want to smile*
*If it takes just a little while*
*Open your eyes and look at the day*
*You'll see things in a different way*
*Don't stop thinking about tomorrow*
*Don't stop, it'll soon be here*
*It'll be here better than before*
*Yesterday's gone, yesterday's gone...*

The lyrics hung in the air, lingering long enough for Cindy to absorb the meaning and smile with hope.

After lunch, we decide to go shopping for frames to decorate Cindy's wall with family photos. We found a 'Family' collage frame at a store nearby. I asked Cindy if I should leave it with her, but she instantly encouraged me to take it home and return it once I had a chance to fill it with photos of her with her daughter, Paige. I needed this project as much as she did, and in one look, we both recognized that.

Cindy walked me to my car, and we hugged and said goodbye. As I was about to step away, Cindy became quiet and looked as if she had something to say. She used to ask for money when we would part ways. Free from addiction, she no longer does. Instead, she reached for my hand, smiled, and said with certainty, "I love you." And with equal affirmation, I replied, "I love you too."

Drivers passed by, locking their doors. Tour companies continue to sell tickets for sightseers to gawk at the homeless. In a neighborhood completely misunderstood, I am reminded of the strength of the human spirit and good that exists within all. A dose of the Downtown Eastside is exactly what I needed.

*"The opposite of addiction isn't sobriety; it's connection."*
*Johann Hari*

# Chapter 16
## Forgiveness

*"As I walked out the door toward the gate that would lead to my freedom, I knew if I didn't leave my bitterness and hatred behind, I'd still be in prison."* Nelson Mandela

### Understanding the Past

In chapter one, I mentioned that my high school principal at the time, Mary, would often help prepare meals and volunteer in the shelter with me. Mary was the one who gave me permission to start *Project HELLO* with students in 2009. She was my boss, my mentor and my friend. We had the pleasure of working together for years in my role as a high school counselor and as a high school vice-principal. Working side by side every day, we knew each other extremely well. Mary knew my family and knew my story.

Years into our working relationship, Mary and I accepted an invitation to attend a card-making class in the evening at a local elementary school. We drove together and chatted about life. When we arrived, we both recognized other attendees, so we went our separate ways to say hello. One of my friends from high school, who is also a teacher, introduced me to her colleague, and in doing so, used my maiden name (Strickland) instead of my married name. Mary, who was across the room, stopped suddenly and stared at me with wonder. She walked over and smiled at me with a look that said she had something profound to say. "I never connected the dots! Your dad's name is Bill, isn't it?" Mary knew that my dad had been absent from my life. In all the time we had known each other, I had never used his name. "I can't believe I didn't realize this until now. Growing up, your dad was my next-door neighbor. His twin sister Barbara was my sister's best friend."

During my dad's childhood, both of his sisters died. His older sister Rae died of cancer at the age of 17, and his twin sister Barbara drank weed killer and committed suicide at age 16. Mary continued, "I remember the pain my family experienced when Barbara died. I saw how it impacted my family and yours. This is the reason I decided to become a teacher and a counselor. After supporting my sister through her grief, I knew I needed to work with youth and try to make a difference. Your aunt's death is the reason I do this work!"

Mary spoke to me about my grandparents and shared how grief had changed them. As parents, they had lost two daughters, and my dad had lost both his sisters. Mary wished I had known my family before they experienced such trauma. She assured me they were kind-hearted and loving people. Grief changed them.

Like the men and women on the streets, my dad had a story. A story of pain and trauma. A story he never moved past. On June 30th, 2016, I received a final phone call from the hospital. This time there was no doubt. My dad was dying. I drove to visit one final time. Here is my blog post from that visit.

### Saying Goodbye – July 1, 2016

We are all connected. The bonds we form with friends, family and colleagues give us our identity, a purpose, a reason to love, and a sense of belonging in this world. In my eyes, nothing is more important than human connection. It's what we carry with us, and what we leave behind. Those who don't connect are quickly forgotten, and those who do, live on in memories, stories and impact.

The strength of our connections gives us the courage to walk alone. There are times in life, we do walk alone, and death is certainly one of them. For most, this is a time to be surrounded by friends and family. For my dad, it wasn't.

When we received the third call of the year saying my dad was dying, my brother and I drove to the hospital knowing it would be our final goodbye. My brother arrived first and sat with him alongside my dad's fourth wife, who we barely knew. She smiled and spoke of my dad's inability to tell the truth. She joked about his unpaid parking tickets and let us know her vacation plans were canceled after learning my dad had taken her property tax money and spent it elsewhere. For years, he had pretended to be working, leaving each morning and returning each night, but she eventually learned it was all a lie. She had no idea where he went during the days. Perhaps he was breaking through fences, golfing for free, perhaps he was elsewhere. We will never know.

She spoke of my dad being proud of Jeff and me, and she let me know that they had gone to watch me run with the Olympic Torch in 2010. My dad did not have the courage to step out of the crowd and say hello.

In time, my brother said goodbye and headed back to work. My dad's fourth wife then turned to me and let me know she had two possessions to pass on. She had my grandmother's tea set, and she had a copy of my dad's twin's suicide note. He had kept it all these years. She knew of my work with

*Beyond HELLO* and thought I might want the note to understand my dad better. She then asked me for bus fare, said a simple goodbye and left, mumbling something about needing to feed her cat.

I sat alone with my dad. In that moment, my dad was slightly responsive and able to mumble a few words. He reached for my hand and squeezed it whenever I would say something that would resonate.

It was my time to talk. It was time for raw honestly. I told my dad how much he had hurt us. I told him what it was like to have a father in the same city that never made an effort. I told him that I was angry and disappointed. I told him I wished it had been different. I told him about my amazing children, and my nieces—four grandchildren whom he did not get to know. I also told him I understood that it was shame that got in the way. I spoke of my work on the DTES and the men like Irvin and Ron, who had helped me understand the way men process shame. Sometimes, when people are in darkness, they believe their best gift is stepping away. I assumed this was the narrative my dad had subscribed to. My dad seemed unable to communicate through words, and I struggled to know if he could hear my hurt and forgiveness. I looked away and sat in silence. When I looked back, I saw a tear fall from his eye.

Sitting in the stark hospital room, I realized how alone my dad was. A man with limited connections in this world was dying with few at his side. The hospital had suggested a hospice to provide more comfort and dignity, but the hospice was full, so the standard room in the trauma unit made do.

I sat in the moment, experiencing one final example of polar-opposite parenting. My mom was at home preparing for a huge family reunion the next day. My dad was dying alone.

I let my dad know that I forgave him for the pain he caused. I told him that my wish was for him to find peace just around the corner, as he did not find it in this world. I did not say I love you, as he did not deserve those three words from Jeff or me. I let go of my dad's hand, recognizing his body was no longer mobile. His hand felt heavy as I placed it down at his side. I said goodbye and left. He passed away alone at the hospital at 3 AM the following morning.

For all of us, there are moments we will face alone. But if we live life right, the connections and love we build with others will give us the courage we need to step forward.

*"Human connection is the most vital aspect of our existence. Without the sweet touch of another being, we are lonely stars waiting to shine gloriously."*
*Joe Straynge*

# Chapter 17
## Our Purpose

*"The supreme goal for humanity is not equality, but connection. People can be equal but still be isolated, not feeling the bond that ties them together. When people are connected, they feel woven into each other. You are a part of me; I am a part of you. Love is what makes us one."*
*Melinda Gates*

### One Caring Adult

Every child needs one caring adult to be able to thrive. I am grateful to my mom for being that person. For every ounce of pain my dad gave us, my mom trumped it with kindness and opportunity. My mom's care is the reason I can sit here and write, blessed with experience, education and strength.

My dad's lack of care is the reason I can relate to others in pain. We all feel pain the same way. After listening to the homeless share their stories, I am well aware that my life is only separated by circumstance. We each have a tipping point that can make us or break us. No one chooses a life on the streets. It is always about pain.

People do not thrive when they are left alone. It is up to all of us to reach out and see those who may be forgotten. When we begin to connect with compassion and hear one another's stories, we recognize that we are more alike than different. Our stories unite us. Every person on this planet was born with something to offer. We each have a purpose. This project has helped me find mine. Let's start seeing people for their strengths and finding ways to include those who have been discarded by mainstream society.

When I began this journey, I judged the homeless. I expected to find people who were different than my social group. I was wrong. Instead, I stumbled into an awakening—the realization that we are all one. We all feel the same way, and we all want to be seen. Our most vulnerable citizens have taught me about hope, courage, resilience, community, and most of all, love. Their stories have touched my heart and helped me see the world through new eyes.

Cindy has become a cherished friend. In April of this year, I met up with her to see how her life had changed since reconnecting with her daughter six years ago. Here is the story of our most recent lunch together.

### *She No Longer Asks for Money – Cindy – April 23, 2019*

When I met Cindy six years ago, she hung to a parking meter, asking everyone who passed for spare change. In the early days of our friendship, our visits would often end with a shameful but quiet request for a few dollars. Six years in, Cindy no longer asks for money. Instead, our relationship has become one of mutual respect, and Cindy's purpose has shifted. Cindy no longer wants to be the recipient of handouts. On this particular day, she wanted to join me and make a difference giving to others.

Cindy still lives in a shelter on Hastings Street in an SRO building. Her living space is smaller than most people's bathrooms, but it's enough for Cindy to have a place to sleep and a wall for family photos. She struggles with mobility and walks with a cane to support her ailing body. While her bones may be weaker than when we first met, her smile is brighter, and overall, she looks much healthier. Cindy continues to be in a long-term relationship with her boy-friend Ron and has a good connection to her daughter Paige who phones regularly since we introduced them to one another in 2014.

Cindy continues to be my inspiration and my motivation to go *Beyond HELLO*. She has taught me about courage, resilience and inner beauty. She knows how to connect with people, and she engages in authentic, genuine and meaningful conversation. As Ava, a twelfth-grade student remarked after our lunch, "That was one of the most meaningful conversations I have had in a long time."

Ava and I had arrived early, not knowing what to expect on a rainy Monday following Easter Sunday. The streets were strangely quiet with only a few people scattered in doorways or seeking shelter under tarps or umbrellas. Ava had a natural gift for connecting, and within minutes, women on the streets trusted Ava and opened up when she offered them bags of make-up.

We met Cindy outside her shelter and made our way down Hastings to our favorite diner, *Save-On-Meats*. As we walked, Cindy commented on how nice it was for us to help people and how she would like to do the same. We gave Cindy some bags of make-up, and within seconds she was calling women by name as we passed, offering up nail polish in their favorite colors.

When we sat down to lunch, Cindy and I reflected on the past six years. She was eager to ask about my boys and learn how my life was going. Cindy asked which *Beyond HELLO* story was my favorite from all the people I have met on the

Downtown Eastside. She beamed with pride when I told her that her story is still my favorite. Together we watched a video clip from 2014 of Cindy speaking on the news about her reunion, and she was once again overwhelmed to remember that she made a difference sharing her story.

Cindy showed a genuine interest in Ava over lunch and asked questions about her upcoming graduation and her acceptance to university. Together they looked at photos and discussed indigenous art. Cindy showed Ava her dream-catcher earrings, and Ava showed Cindy a pair of beautifully crafted earrings she planned to wear at graduation. Cindy spoke about the shame she felt dropping out of school at age 14. I reminded her that when we met, she was reading *War and Peace* on a cold side-walk, and her lack of a diploma certainly didn't measure her true intelligence. Cindy was impressed to learn that Ava had written her first children's book, *It's Time to Go,* where a butterfly guides a little boy on his journey seeking asylum in a new country.

As we chatted over breakfast sandwiches, I offered Cindy a meal token for *Save-On-Meats* so she could return at a future time and enjoy another meal. She accepted. I offered a second one, but she asked me to keep it for someone who needed it more. As our meal ended, we headed outside to walk back towards Cindy's shelter. A few steps in, a man struggled with his umbrella and searched the ground for cigarette butts. Cindy approached, put a hand on his shoulder, and asked if he would like her token for a free meal. He gratefully accepted and asked if he could buy a cigarette. Cindy refused his money but reached into her purse and gave him a cigarette. No longer one for handouts,

Cindy smiled ear to ear, helping someone who needed it a little more than she did.

With some hugs and some laughs, we said goodbye to Cindy. Ava and I headed to the car while Cindy headed up Hastings, handing out nail polish to those in need of a friendly smile and a splash of color on an otherwise bleak Vancouver day.

### Together, Let's Go Beyond HELLO

Ten years ago, I sat with the morning paper and came up with a simple idea of how my students and I could help. I planned a one-day field trip and signed my students up for shifts at a local homeless shelter. I had no idea that this simple plan would ripple so far. To date, my students have helped over 700 people in our community reconnect with loved ones through cards, phone calls and face to face reunions at Christmas and Mother's Day. Our cards have reached families across Canada and the United States.

Since 2013, my students have helped me go *Beyond HELLO*, taking people to lunch to hear their stories. Although our stories all take place in Vancouver, BC, I am hopeful we have made an impact beyond our city. My blog posts at www.beyondhello.org, which share stories from the streets, have been viewed over 45,000 times in more than 30 countries. I am hopeful that our project has inspired others in communities around the world to reach out and connect with the forgotten.

This journey has been one of the greatest blessings of my life. People have opened their doors, offered to help and supported our work in ways I could not have dreamed of. I have learned that miracles happen when we listen, pay attention and connect with one another on a soulful level. I am grateful to the men and women who have opened their hearts and shared their stories.

People who are homeless have lost everything, but rock bottom has graced them with the wisdom to appreciate what matters. I have learned about hope, courage, and resilience. I have learned that nothing matters more than connecting and loving one another. I have found forgiveness and healed my own soul. In a journey meant to help, I have gained so much more than I could ever give.

I hope the stories from the streets will inspire you to go *Beyond HELLO*. I hope you live with a new awareness and see those who others have forgotten. I hope you say hello to a neighbor you have yet to meet, buy a coffee for a stranger, invite the custodian at work to tell you their story, or find the courage to repair a broken relationship from your past. Listen attentively and discover that we are all more alike than different. See the invisible. Go *Beyond HELLO*, connect with compassion, and together let's rekindle the human spirit, one conversation a time.

*"Eventually, you will come to understand that love heals everything, and love is all there is."*
*Gary Zukav*

# Acknowledgments

I could not have walked this journey alone. Mom, thanks for telling me to talk to strangers and raising me to be creative and confident. Mary, thank you for saying yes to *Project HELLO* when I told you about my crazy idea. To all my students and colleagues who have helped with *Project HELLO* and *Beyond HELLO*, this is your story too. Your compassion, generosity and willingness to help others has allowed over 700 families to connect. I am grateful and proud of you.

Shawn, Jaden and Cole: thank you for joining me on the streets, being patient with me and encouraging me along the way. To my husband Shawn, thank you for your love and support and thank you for reminding me for ten years that I had a story to write. Jaden and Cole, thanks for keeping me laughing. I cannot wait to see your future unfold.

Thank you to my friends who have joined me with *Project HELLO*, read my blog, supported me and encouraged me to keep writing. A special thank you to Julie and Cheryl for your help editing, and Jen for choosing the fictional names for the book to protect the confidentiality of our most vulnerable citizens. Thank you to Kyra and Todd Schaefer from As You Wish Publishing for believing in my story. You spark joy, and I am grateful to have you as my publishers and friends.

Finally, thank you to the men and women on the streets of Vancouver for trusting me with your stories, opening your hearts and showing vulnerability. You have taught me about courage, resilience and grit. Noelle, you were the heart of the DTES, and your smile helped so many. Ron, thank you for being wonderful to my boys. Irvin, thanks for teaching me the power of connecting a community, and Cindy, thank you for teaching us all that miracles can happen. Never give up on love.

I dream of a day, where no one is pushed away, and the fringe of society is invited back in. I dream of a day where we all connect with compassion and see the beauty within one another. To everyone who has taken time to read my story, I hope you walk through life with your eyes open looking for those who are invisible and seeking out the forgotten. We are meant to connect. Please reach out and go *Beyond HELLO*. Together, let's rekindle the human spirit one conversation at a time.

# About The Author

Kristi Blakeway is a school principal in Maple Ridge, BC, where she lives with her husband and two sons. She is the founder of Beyond HELLO, a TEDx Speaker, Olympic Torchbearer and winner of the YWCA Women of Distinction Award for Connecting Community. Kristi encourages everyone to step outside their comfort zone, engage in soulful conversation, and connect with compassion. A storyteller at heart, she blogs regularly at www.beyondhello.org.